ROUTLEDGE LIBRARY EDITIONS:
PRISON AND PRISONERS

Volume 5

THE ENGLISH PRISONS

THE ENGLISH PRISONS

Their Past and Their Future

D. L. HOWARD

Routledge
Taylor & Francis Group

LONDON AND NEW YORK

First published in 1960 by Methuen & Co Ltd

This edition first published in 2024
by Routledge
4 Park Square, Milton Park, Abingdon, Oxon OX14 4RN

and by Routledge
605 Third Avenue, New York, NY 10158

Routledge is an imprint of the Taylor & Francis Group, an informa business

British Library Cataloguing in Publication Data
A catalogue record for this book is available from the British Library

ISBN: 978-1-032-55549-2 (Set)
ISBN: 978-1-032-56691-7 (Volume 5) (hbk)
ISBN: 978-1-032-56698-6 (Volume 5) (pbk)
ISBN: 978-1-003-43682-9 (Volume 5) (ebk)

DOI: 10.4324/9781003436829

Publisher's Note
The publisher has gone to great lengths to ensure the quality of this reprint but points out that some imperfections in the original copies may be apparent.

Disclaimer
The publisher has made every effort to trace copyright holders and would welcome correspondence from those they have been unable to trace.

The English Prisons

THEIR PAST AND THEIR FUTURE

by

D. L. HOWARD

LONDON

METHUEN & CO LTD

36 ESSEX STREET . WC2

First published 1960
© *1960 by D. L. Howard*
Printed and bound in Great Britain
by Butler & Tanner Ltd
Frome & London
Cat. No. 2/6358/1

FOR ELISABETH
AND OUR FRIENDS
IN THE PRISON AND
BORSTAL SERVICE

CONTENTS

vii

viii   CONTENTS

ILLUSTRATIONS

PLATES

LINE DRAWINGS IN TEXT

Permission to reproduce the illustrations has been kindly given as follows: Royal Netherlands Embassy, London, Nos 1, 2; Central Office of Information, Nos 7a, 8; Radio Times Hulton Picture Library, Nos 3, 4, 5, 6, 7b, and pages 44 and 46; County Archivist, East Sussex County Council: Appendix A: The New Prison, Lewes

'*The mood and temper of the public in regard to the treatment of crime and criminals is one of the most unfailing tests of any country. A calm, dispassionate recognition of the rights of the accused, and even of the convicted criminal, against the State – a constant heart-searching by all charged with the duty of punishment – a desire and eagerness to rehabilitate in the world of industry those who have paid their due in the hard coinage of punishment: tireless efforts towards the discovery of curative and regenerative processes: unfailing faith that there is a treasure, if you can only find it, in the heart of every man. These are the symbols, which, in the treatment of crime and criminal, mark and measure the stored up strength of a nation, and are sign and proof of the living virtue within it.*'

WINSTON S. CHURCHILL
speaking in the House of Commons as
Home Secretary, 20th July 1910

INTRODUCTION

The first part of this book surveys the history of imprisonment in England from the end of the eighteenth century to the present day. It describes changes in the design and administration of prisons and the attitudes ordinary men and women had to these developments.

In Part Two of the book I have described some of the many problems which have still to be solved if we want to make sure that by imprisoning offenders against the law we are really going to help them as individuals and thereby reduce the incidence of crime. More crimes were recorded in 1959 than at any other time since such records were first kept in 1893. If we are to be more successful in dealing with the problem of crime in the future than we have been in the past, we must devise some more effective form of institutional treatment for known offenders than simple imprisonment. We may continue to call the institutions of the future by the name of prison; the treatment applied in them must be quite different from that which the name implies today.

There are signs that profound changes will take place in the organization of the prison service of England and Wales in the near future. If they are to be effective they will require much more money than we have yet been accustomed to spending on prisons, and a more informed interest on the part of the public, not only in what happens to a man once he has been sentenced in court and pushed through the prison gates, but also in the social difficulties ex-prisoners, women as well as men, have to face when newly released. I hope that this book, which is intended for the general reader as well as for serious students of penal history, may help to awaken such an interest.

The nineteenth century imposed harsh and brutal treatments upon prisoners in the name of our society, but it also saw the gradual ascendance of the reformative, rehabilitative spirit which pervades much of the work done in dreadfully old-fashioned and ill-equipped buildings by the Prison Service today. The many devoted and idealistic people now at work in the Prison Service need facilities which will help rather than hinder them in their efforts, but above all they need encouragement and understanding from the public as a whole, who will benefit from their success in the future.

My wife (formerly Elisabeth Rée), who is Deputy Secretary of the Howard League, has given me enormous help in assembling and interpreting much of the material in this book. I am also grateful to Mr S. G. Clarke, now Governor of Liverpool Prison, under whom I had the privilege and pleasure of working as Tutor Organizer in the large open prison at Eastchurch, Kent. Mr Clarke read and commented upon my original draft of Part One of the book, and made many helpful suggestions.

I have been greatly helped, too, by Mr Leslie Fairweather, A.R.I.B.A., who has most generously allowed me to use his valuable thesis, *The Design of Penal Institutions*, which is now in the Library of the Howard League for Penal Reform. Mr Fairweather's work can be warmly commended to all who seek information and comment upon the development of prison buildings in western Europe and the United States of America in the past, and on the future of prison design in this country.

I give my warm thanks also to Mr Hugh Klare, who, as Secretary of the Howard League, has never spared himself in giving encouragement and advice to those interested in crime and its prevention, in any capacity. Many men and women who have fallen foul of the law, and many who have tried to help them in the Prison Service, will be permanently in Mr Klare's debt.

The ideas expressed in Part Two of this book are by no means all my own. They have been assimilated over many years, from conversations with very many people: with academic criminologists in England and abroad, with probation officers, ex-prisoners, members of the Howard League and men and women in all ranks of the Prison Service. Many have come from books and articles I have read and reviewed in the ten years since I first became interested in the criminal and the problems involved in treating him. If I have by chance put forward an idea first introduced to me in conversation or in a forgotten article, and have used it without making acknowledgement, I beg the forgiveness of its originator. I would also like to thank all those who have kindly given permission for the use of quotations from their books. In each case, the source of the quotation is given. The opinions expressed throughout the book are my own, and I do not claim perfection for any of my proposals.

In conclusion, I wish to express my respect and admiration for the work of Dr Hermann Mannheim, O.B.E., one of the greatest of modern criminologists and one of the pioneers of criminological research in this country. As Reader in the subject at the London School of Economics, Dr Mannheim has introduced many hundreds of undergraduates, including myself, to the study of criminology and has stimulated and encouraged much outstanding work of investigation into the causes and treatment of crime.

D. L. HOWARD,
1959

Danemead
Cranbrook
Kent

PART ONE

Our Prisons in the Past

'Those darling bygone times, Mr Carker, with their delicious fortresses and their dear old dungeons and their delightful places of torture and their romantic vengeances and their picturesque assaults and sieges and everything that makes life truly charming. How dreadfully we have degenerated.'

'Yes, we have fallen off deplorably,' said Mr Carker.

CHARLES DICKENS
Dombey and Son

CHAPTER I

THE EARLY PRISONS

The punishment of criminal and political offenders by confining them in prisons is a modern practice, but prisons as places of detention are common to most societies throughout history. *Genesis* tells us of Joseph's imprisonment in Egypt two thousand years before the birth of Christ, and there are references to large underground chambers used as prisons in Greek Literature of the seventh century B.C. But Plato, when he said

> Let there be prisons in the city, one for the safe keeping of persons awaiting trial and sentence, another for the amendment of disorderly persons and vagrants, those guilty of misdemeanours . . . , a third to be situated away from the habitations of man and to be used for the *punishment* of the felon . . .

was anticipating the penal systems of modern western European countries by many hundreds of years.

The use of prisons, not as a means of punishment in themselves, but as a way of ensuring safe custody, was established in Roman Law by Justinian in the fifth century B.C. The typical Roman prison was an underground cellar to which access was made from a small grating covering the top. An example of this kind, now known as the Mamertine Prison, still exists in Rome, near the Capitoline Hill. It consists of an upper rectangular room lit only by a hole in the roof, with a dome-shaped dungeon below. The prisoners were confined to the upper room unless condemned to death, when they would be thrown into the lower dungeon to starve, to be strangled, or to await an even more painful and lingering death.

Imprisonment as a form of punishment was used in a few cases in Saxon England. The laws of Aethelstan stipulated that a person convicted of murder should be thrust into prison for one hundred

3

and twenty days before he might be claimed by his kinsmen. A penalty of imprisonment for perjury in a Grand Assize was introduced by Henry II, and Henry III instituted a punishment of one year's imprisonment for infringement of the forest law. In the last half of the thirteenth century Edward I used imprisonment extensively, but mainly to induce confession or to ensure the payment of fines.

The ecclesiastical authorities made use of prisons as places of punishment in the thirteenth century mainly because they were not allowed to impose death penalties. George Ives[1] tells of an unfortunate monk who had bitten his prior's finger like a dog, whereupon the prior was ordered by his bishop to put the offender '... in prison under iron chains in which he shall be content with bread, indifferent ales, pottage, and a pittance of meat or fish (which on the sixth day he shall do without) until he is penitent'. During the Inquisition, Pope Gregory IX gave orders that all who were converted to the faith after arrest because of fear of death should be imprisoned for life. This imprisonment varied from complete cellular isolation in some ecclesiastical prisons, to communal life with only occasional withdrawal to a cell in others. Then, as in the eighteenth century, there was much free association of prisoners with one another, and 'grafting' was regularly practised by gaolers, who kept money belonging to inmates and often ordered supplies of food for prisoners who had long been dead.

Throughout our history we have shown remarkable ingenuity in devising and inflicting punishments upon our fellow-men. Rather less imagination has been devoted to the development of effective reformative measures, even in those rare and brief periods when there has been some popular support for ideas of inducing the offender to conform by educational and therapeutic means, instead of making him suffer for his wrongs. With few exceptions, such as those already quoted, the medieval prison, filthy and disease-ridden though it was, had the character of a waiting-room. Those who survived illness and sadistic torture eventually emerged to receive the official penalty for their offences.

Death penalties were most common and most painfully carried out during the Middle Ages. The infliction of death by breaking at the wheel, drowning, impaling, boiling in oil and burning, was

[1] *A History of Penal Methods* (New York, 1914).

regularly practised in medieval times for small offences. In general, the frequency with which capital punishment was imposed declined towards the end of this period. Thus, impaling and immuring were abolished in Switzerland in 1399, and death by drowning was abandoned as a penal method in the same country in 1615. In Frankfort the number of executions fell from 317 in the fifteenth century, to 248 in the sixteenth and 140 in the seventeenth.[1] But in England this tendency was reversed. There were only 17 offences for which the death penalty could be awarded in the first part of the fifteenth century, but the number rose to 200 in 1820. Nevertheless, between 1813 and 1819 only 10·5 per cent. of the death sentences passed in English courts were actually carried out, and in the period from 1827 to 1833 the number of actual capital punishments fell to only 4·1 per cent. of those prescribed by the courts. The increase in the severity of the penal code in this country at the end of the eighteenth century was due partly to the extremely unsettling effect upon English society of the industrial changes of the time.

Together with the death penalty, social degradation in many forms was applied as a punishment in medieval times. Shame and humiliation were inflicted upon criminals by physical mutilation, branding and torture, often carried out in public, or, more mildly, by use of the ducking-stool, the pillory and the stocks. The 'brank' was a device placed over the head of the offender like a parrot's cage, with a bar which was thrust into the mouth, holding down the tongue with sharp spikes and thus effectively preventing any attempts to speak or to cry out. These implements were still in vogue in the sixteenth and seventeenth centuries, and provided much popular amusement. But they often failed to accomplish their purpose. A law of 1698, providing for branding on the cheek, was repealed after only eight years because it had not had 'its desired effect of deterring offenders from the further committing of crimes and offences, but, on the contrary, such offenders, being rendered thereby unfit to be entrusted in any service or employment to get their livelihood in any honest and lawful way, became the more desperate'.[2]

Physical torture inflicted specifically as a punishment in itself has been widely practised in most societies. The cutting off of feet,

---

[1] Kriegk, G. L., *Deutsches Bürgerthum in Mittelalters*, Vol. I.
[2] Pike, L. O., *A History of Crime in England*, Vol. II (London, 1873–1876).

the burning out of eyes, removal of ears, nose or upper lip, and even scalping, were practised in Saxon England, 'so that punishment be inflicted and the soul preserved'. These penalties disappeared in England when public feeling turned against them and could be expressed. Just as the death penalty, once awarded, was not always carried out in early nineteenth-century England, transportation finding favour as an apparently more humane alternative, so the infliction of torture gradually became merely symbolic. Bentham, in his *Principles of Penal Law*, could write at the end of the eighteenth century:

> Burning in the hand, according as the criminal and the executioner can agree, is performed either with a cold or a red hot iron; and if it be a red hot iron, it is only a slice of ham which is burnt; to complete the farce, the criminal screams, whilst it is only the fat which smokes and burns, and the knowing spectators only laugh at this parody of justice.

Nevertheless, Blackstone, in attempting to show how much more humane the eighteenth century was than the Middle Ages, had to point out that occasionally those who were about to be hanged were now dragged to the scaffold on hurdles, and not, to the greater entertainment of the crowds who gathered to witness these ceremonies, pulled directly along the roads with only their ragged clothing to soften the impact of the rutted ground. Disembowelling was still practised for some offences, and physical mutilation was still commonplace, even at the end of the seventeenth century. With majestic equality, these punishments applied not only to women as well as men, but also to small children. But the largest proportion of the prison population in eighteenth-century England was not formed by offenders awaiting these treatments; it was made up of debtors, confined at the will of their creditors until they or their friends could pay the money – often a paltry sum – which was owing. The period of waiting for trial was usually a long one, and it might amount to a year after a man's first confinement before the local Assize Court met to deal with him. The longer a prisoner was held awaiting jurisdiction, the more unlikely was it that he would ever be released into freedom. At Hull Prison an exceptional case occurred: there the Assizes were held only once every seven years, and a murderer was released after three years' imprisonment because the main witness against him had died in the interval. Not only were prisoners in the eighteenth century ill fed and housed in un-hygienic, frequently damp accommodation while awaiting trial, without medical attention; they also had to pay for the treatment thus endured. A man found innocent after trial would almost certainly, if he were poor, remain a prisoner *in debt to the gaol-keepers* until he died of fever or, much more rarely, until a relative came along to pay for him. Such a man would not receive much encouragement from his gaolers to live on, consuming even the most meagre allowance of prison food. This was the reason for the first insistence by John Howard, the greatest of all prison reformers, that penitentiaries should not be in the charge of un-paid officials. One of the first (though unsuccessful) requests that Howard made on becoming Sheriff of Bedfordshire was that the local prison keeper should be paid a wage from the county rates.[1]

In the middle of the eighteenth century most county authorities were responsible for the prisons in their capital towns, but almost as many (no one in England at this time was quite sure of the total number of prisons in the country) were in private hands. The Duke of Leeds owned Halifax Prison, and a Mr J. R. Walters possessed one at Exeter. Lord Derby drew an income of £13 a year from Macclesfield Prison. None was a building especially designed for the purpose, unless the medieval dungeons of Chester Castle and other old fortresses still in use could be regarded as such. Gate-houses in city walls were frequently used. Where prison walls were tumbling down, or a lack of bars at the windows made it easy for prisoners to escape, an answer was found in per-manently chaining the inmates. So heavily were they loaded with irons that walking or even lying down to sleep was difficult and painful. The practice of chaining was fairly common even in the most secure institutions, because 'county gaolers do sometimes grant dispensations, and indulge their prisoners, men as well as women, with what they call "choice of irons", if they pay for it.[2] At Ely Prison, the property of the Bishop, Howard found men fixed to the floor on their backs by heavy irons.

Very often the owner of a gaol did not run it himself. The right

[1] A Bill to make this possible was introduced in the House of Commons by Alexander Popham in 1773, at Howard's instigation. The Bill was unsuccessful.

[2] Howard, J., *The State of the Prisons* (1777). For a full account of John Howard's life and work, see Howard, D. L., *John Howard: Prison Reformer* (London, Christopher Johnson, 1958).

to do so was farmed out to a local man who recouped by extortion, charging excessively for better food than that normally issued, for the privilege of walking without chains, or for fresh water. Special charges were even made for 'turning the key' when a prisoner was released. There was no inspection of prisons by the government, by the county authorities or any other official body. Any method, cruel or kind, could be employed by gaolers to augment their incomes, without critical comment. No questions were asked when a prisoner died. Indeed, for many of those who escaped capital punishment, death might have seemed preferable to the utter misery of mind and body which constituted existence in prison. More men died from fever in gaols in the eighteenth century, after a few months of stifling, hungry life, than were ever legally put to death each year on the scaffold. For those who lived in the unventilated, overcrowded prisons, where even straw to lie upon was rarely provided, the gaoler was an all-powerful monster, skilled in torment. Gaolers were 'frequently a merciless race of men, and by being conversant with scenes of misery, steeled against any tender sensation', says Blackstone.

Attempts to improve this state of affairs were not unknown before Howard came on the scene. The Society for the Promotion of Christian Knowledge made an investigation into London prisons in 1702, but its exhaustive proposals were never published. A government committee under General Oglethorpe, appointed in 1729 to examine the gaols of the entire kingdom, also had little effect, although its report[1] informed the House of Commons that 'the more dismal and shocking was the scene of cruelty, barbarity and extortion' the farther the committee went in its investigations. Oglethorpe secured the establishment of another committee in 1754 to inquire into the vicious practices 'and every kind of irregularity' then common in the King's Bench Prison.[2] A Bill providing for the complete rebuilding of this institution was passed in the following year. Henry Fielding, in his novels,

[1] *House of Commons Journal*, XXXVI.

[2] Three London Prisons, the Fleet, Marshalsea and the King's Bench Prison, all chiefly for debtors, came directly under the King's Court at Westminster. They might therefore be regarded as the responsibility of the central government in London. They were combined into one institution in 1842. The Savoy Palace, used as a military detention barracks in the eighteenth century, was also directly under Parliamentary control, in theory at least. The Tower of London, another national prison, was rarely used after the earliest years of the eighteenth century.

makes some pointed references to prison conditions, which he deplores, but there are few other indications of lively interest in the sufferings of criminal offenders in the years before 1773 when Howard began his work.

John Howard's influence on the design and administration of prisons throughout the world is quite unrivalled, and his proposals, revolutionary in his own day, greatly influenced the way in which the large walled prisons of nineteenth-century England were administered and designed. But although Howard's revelations startled the reading public when he first made them, little improvement took place for many years after his death. The nineteenth century in English penal history was a period of slow adaptation to Howard's ideals: an adaptation which only approached completion when all prisons were placed in the hands of a central body of Prison Commissioners in 1877, and which in some respects has not been fully achieved even today.

Howard's proposals for prison reform have become so deeply entrenched in modern practice that they may seem commonplace to our eyes. He not only had to plead for the good regulation of prisons: he had to demand first of all that regulation *of some kind* should be commonly applied to gaols in an England where many were profitable businesses, none was governed by any standard rules, and none was subject to independent inspection. The charge placed against nearly all penal reformers since his day, that they would make gaols so pleasant that criminals would strive to get into them, was first made familiar to him. Nevertheless, deprivation of liberty, no matter how humane the conditions in which it is enforced, remains today as great a deterrent as it was in the eighteenth century.

The chaotic conditions prevailing in English prisons in his day are revealed by the briefest glance at Howard's proposals for reform. He asked for the segregation of offenders by age and sex and according to the severity of the crimes they had committed. He wanted cellular confinement, so that moral and physical contagion would be reduced to a minimum. He asked for a salaried staff to be appointed in all prisons, so that gaolers would have no need to resort to extortion or overworking of their charges to secure a reasonable living; he demanded the appointment of chaplains and medical officers to relieve the spiritual degradation endured in prison and to overcome gaol fever (typhus) and the other diseases rife in prisons. He wanted the sale of alcohol to inmates forbidden, and asked for the men and women (and the children they bore in prison) to be properly clothed, not left in the slowly rotting dress they wore on arrival, and he wanted prisoners to be fed sufficiently well to maintain their health and life. To reduce all Howard's proposals to a minimum, what he asked for was a sensible, humane programme of treatment, applied indiscriminately to all men and women sent to prison: a programme which would ensure that they were no worse in bodily or mental health on discharge than they were on reception. The introduction of any one of John Howard's ideas in an eighteenth-century prison would have been startlingly original.

No complete picture of the evils regularly practised in prisons up and down the country, nor any considered plan to alleviate them generally, was put before Parliament until Howard was called upon to give evidence before the whole House in March 1774. Even this performance, although Howard was called back and formally thanked for his voluntary work by the Commons, had little immediate effect. Parliament was unwilling to tackle the enormously complex problem of reorganizing the penal facilities of the country at that time. It was not aware how many gaols existed, and no doubt many individual Members realized that powerful interests in their constituencies would be offended by any attempt to make a clean sweep of all the abuses. Until 1759, when they had provided that creditors who put men in prison for debt should allow them fourpence a day for maintenance, the Commons had been content with an occasional *Insolvent Act*, stipulating that all debtors confined on a particular day should be released.

Some measure of the ineffectiveness of Parliament in the field of domestic legislation at this time is given by Howard's discovery, fifteen years after the law of 1759 had been enacted, that only a small proportion of debtors were in fact receiving their daily fourpences. Even had the Act been universally applied, as Parliament had intended that it should be, it could not have been very useful, for the groat was quickly taken from debtors by their gaolers on a variety of pretexts. The same Act had also made an unsuccessful attempt to abolish *garnish*, the practice whereby prisoners took money, clothing or any other property from a new inmate under threat of using physical violence upon him. That they should gather together in their rags or nakedness to divest a new-comer was inevitable: no other way of obtaining clothing was open to them.

Some distinction must be recognized at this stage between the county gaols ('common gaols') and the houses of correction, at least in their origins. The first were under the charge of a public authority: the municipal corporations in towns which were counties in their own right, or the County Sheriffs (representing the King, but only in legal tradition) in the counties proper. Their administration had from common practice come to be regarded as the private concern of the keepers, who were expected to make a profit from the business of running them. Bridewells and houses of correction were legally under the direct jurisdiction of Justices of the Peace. In origin they were not penal institutions, but part of a national scheme for the relief of destitution. In the intention of the Act of 1576, which established houses of correction, they were to be rather like a modern workhouse, where vagrants and the unemployed were put to work (in circumstances by no means pleasant) partly to reform them and implant in them 'a taste for industry', and partly to deter others from following their example. Justices in Quarter Sessions were required to appoint a Master or Governor from each house and pay him a salary. It was not unusual, until the end of the seventeenth century, for the inmates to be paid for their labours as well.

At first, houses of correction were fairly successful. It was believed, and with some justification, that a man sent to one of them would come out better for his experience. But by the beginning of the eighteenth century the character of the houses had changed into that of a common gaol. This may have been the result of well-meaning attempts by some magistrates to save young offenders from the contamination of prison life by sending them instead to institutions which were well known to have a salutary effect on the character. Slowly, the houses of correction and the common gaols became identified together in the public mind and even the Justices themselves overlooked any distinction in their origins. In 1720 this identity was legally recognized under a statute which allowed the Justices to commit idlers either to the gaols or to the houses of correction, as they might think fit. 'In the early part of the eighteenth century it became, in fact, in most counties, difficult to discover any practical distinction between the house of correction and the common gaol', say the Webbs.[1]

Wakefield Prison, to which the training school of the modern Prison Service is at present attached, had its origin as a house of correction. Much interesting material relating to its development is housed in the museum attached to the school.

[1] Webb, Sidney and Beatrice, *English Prisons under Local Government* (London, 1922).

CHAPTER II

CONFUSION AND COUNSEL

'... if it were the aim and wish of Magistrates to effect the destruction, present and future, of young delinquents, they could not desire a more effectual method than to confine them in our prisons.'

JOHN HOWARD

After John Howard had given evidence to the House of Commons, two Bills introduced under his influence by Alexander Popham were passed into law. The first established that a prisoner set free by the courts should be allowed to return home without payment of the discharge fee asked for by his keepers. The second attempted again to deal with gaol fever by 'authorizing and requiring' Justices of the Peace to have the walls of prison wards scraped and whitewashed at least once a year. But as we have already noted, Parliamentary decisions were not inevitably translated into action at this time. The new laws were ignored nearly everywhere. In the notes of his visits to English and Welsh prisons in 1775, Howard remarks on the ignorance of some county gaolers of the new legislation, and on the refusal of others, aware of the laws, to carry them out. Without an inspectorate to visit prisons regularly and report on the way they were being run, any regulations Parliament might lay down could be safely shunned.

Fortunately, two men of greater influence than Popham, Sir William Eden (later Baron Auckland) and Sir William Blackstone, had been impressed by Howard's ideas, and saw in them a possible answer to the problem which would be created if loss of the American colonies made transportation of criminals overseas impossible.

It had long been a practice to deport convicted men to whom the death sentence was inapplicable to penal settlements in the colonies across the Atlantic, where labour had been badly needed before the slave trade from West Africa was well developed. The prisoners concerned were in theory granted pardons subject to their acceptance of transportation. Certain classes of offenders had been liable to 'banishment from the realm' since the time of Elizabeth I, but the first record of transportation to the Americas is from the reign of James I, who decreed that 100 'dissolute' men should be transported to Virginia. Cromwell also made use of the principle to send his political enemies as slaves or indented servants to the plantations of the West Indies. In 1679 the practice was established in Statute Law as applying to all classes of offenders who escaped execution. An Act of 1767 further defined transportation as a penal instrument. From then onward many of those found guilty of capital offences were only nominally sentenced to death, and then put in the hands of private contractors who undertook to transport them across the ocean like live cattle.

Out of 1,066 offenders sentenced to death in 1824, only 40 were in fact executed. A new and profitable form of business connected with the penal system had grown up. Contractors were given use of the convicts' labour for seven or fourteen years, and could sell this valuable property to settlers hungry for labour on their farms, at auctions held immediately the transport ships arrived at American ports. So great was the demand for convict labour in the early years of the system that great crowds would surge round the docks as soon as the ships arrived, and bidding was furious. Mercantile returns of these sales show that the average price for an able man at the auctions was twenty pounds. Women fetched a smaller sum. Having acquired labour so expensively, many settlers were determined to get the maximum value for their money, and for thousands of convicts life in America was brief and brutish in consequence.

In 1776 the government was forced to stop transportation and find alternative means of disposal. Parliament had suddenly discovered, in the face of rebellion in the colonies, that 'Transportation to His Majesty's colonies and plantations in America [is] found to be attended by various inconveniences, particularly by depriving the kingdom of many subjects whose labour might be useful to the community . . .' (16 Geo. III). An Act was then passed, stipulating that prisoners sentenced to or made liable for transportation should be made available for certain hard labour until satisfactory alternative means of dealing with them could be found. Blackstone and Eden together, adopting Howard's principles, took this as an opportunity for proposing the development of at least one national penitentiary in which men could do heavy labouring work but remain in solitary cellular confinement when at rest. While performing tasks 'of the hardest and most servile kind, for which drudgery is chiefly required', they would be closely supervised to make sure that no intercourse of any kind took place between them. This proposal became law in the Penitentiary Houses Act of 1779, in which we can see the origins of the sentence of hard labour which so dominated English penal methods towards the end of the nineteenth century. The Act optimistically hopes that

if any offenders convicted of crimes for which transportation has been usually inflicted were ordered to solitary confinement, accompanied by well-regulated hard labour, and religious instruction, it might be the means, under Providence, not only of deterring others, but also of reforming the individuals, and turning them to habits of industry.

The four points Howard had particularly stressed, of systematic inspection, adequate sanitation, security of buildings and abolition of fees, would be recognized in the new penitentiary. There would also be, as Howard had demanded there should, an adequate and regular supply of food and simple clothing for the men. Religious services would take place in the new prison, and attendance at them would be compulsory. The first prison to be erected in Britain in accordance with this Act - and the last, although Blackstone and Eden had envisaged several - was not begun until well into the nineteenth century, and the delay in building it was one for which Howard must be partially blamed.

Three supervisors were appointed under the Act of 1779 to decide on a site for the new penitentiary and to supervise its erection. Howard was one of them, but he accepted the post only on condition that a friend of his, Dr Fothergill, should also be appointed. He rigidly insisted that the site should be in Islington, and Fothergill supported this contention. Whatley, the third member, was equally enthusiastic about building the gaol on land in Limehouse. Howard argued that no situation could be more appropriate than Islington, apart from one nearer the river, and that no land close to the Thames could be found. Since Whatley's site was closer to the Thames than Howard's, and Millbank Penitentiary was built on the very edge of the water only a few years afterwards, it is hard to follow the reformer's reasoning in this matter. Indeed, the incident illustrates an unsatisfactory aspect of Howard's character, revealed repeatedly throughout his life: his desire always to dominate in argument, and his inability to co-operate as a member of a team. He refused offers of arbitration and resigned from the board of supervisors, thereby allowing the scheme for a national penitentiary to slumber for over twenty years. When it was eventually built, the grandiose architectural ideas of Jeremy Bentham had caught the official imagination, and its design owed more to him than to Howard.

Had Howard adopted a more reasonable attitude he might have been able to make the temporary cessation of transportation permanent, by encouraging and hastening the production of an alternative. But the delay he caused led the government to invoke the Act of 1776 already quoted, which Howard had strongly opposed when it passed through the Commons. It was now decided that offenders who might otherwise have been sent to the new penitentiary should be sentenced to a period of hard labour on the embankments in the lower reaches of the Thames and in other estuaries throughout the kingdom. In sheer desperation to find accommodation of some kind for the type of men hitherto transported, the statute was amended so that they could be confined in hulks actually moored in the rivers where they were to work. Officially, these prisoners were still sentenced to transportation, on the assumption that a depository in another part of the world would become available for them. An experiment had been made with penal settlements on the coast of West Africa, despite the fatal character of the climate. But only a few men were sent there, and, says Griffiths,[1]

> the statesmen of the day had fully recognized that they had no right to increase the punishment of imprisonment by making it also capital; and the government, despairing of finding a suitable place of exile, were about to commit themselves (once again) to the plan of home penitentiaries, when the discoveries of Captain Cook in the South Seas drew attention to the vast territories of Australasia . . .

[1] Griffiths, A., *Memorials of Millbank* (London, Chapman & Hall, 1884).

A Panopticon prison at Breda, Holland, erected 1901

It was not until 1787 that the government was able to revert with relief to transportation of the old kind, using the newly discovered southern continent. In the meantime, large, overcrowded, floating prisons had been created in the Thames, at Portsmouth, Plymouth and in other large ports, in which all the evils of the common gaols were grossly exaggerated. The hulks quickly achieved an evil reputation. They were the most inhumane penitentiaries in existence.[1] The lapse of ten years, during which actual transportation overseas had fallen to the merest trickle, meant more and more discarded ships were brought into service as prison hulks, and since men continued to be sentenced in large numbers the hulks remained grotesquely overcrowded for many years after the new settlements in Australia came into use.

The Act of 1779 was not completely forgotten. This had already recorded the government's view that cellular confinement (as proposed by Howard) was desirable in a national penitentiary, and some very forward-looking county authorities had soon secured local Acts permitting them to establish it in their own prisons. But the principle was not to be generally adopted in England until the middle of the nineteenth century. Then, ironically, the idea came back to Britain from the now independent American colonies where it had been successfully used in Philadelphia.[2] Pentonville Prison, erected in 1842, was a model institution designed specifically for cellular confinement.

In 1791 the M.P. for Northampton, Powis, then leading the prison reformers in the House of Commons (and no doubt considerably stimulated by the local Acts instituting separation), secured the passage of a *General Prisons Act*. This was to apply the main features of the national penitentiary scheme to all common gaols, bridewells and houses of correction in England and Wales. Justices were required to make rules applying to their own prisons similar to those envisaged for a national prison in Blackstone and Eden's Act of 1779. Moreover, Justices were to inspect these institutions regularly and report their findings *in writing* to the Quarter Sessions. Unfortunately this measure, like so many others of the eighteenth century, was ineffective in practice. The Act implied that local prisons should receive men sentenced to

---

[1] For a full account of the prison ships, see Branch-Johnson, W., *The English Prison Hulks* (London, Christopher Johnson, 1957).
[2] See Chapter VIII.

C

hard labour for long periods, but the prison buildings of the provinces were quite unsuitable for this purpose and there was no willingness on the part of the Justices concerned to bear the expense of rebuilding them or adapting them. From 1791 onward it was not the absence of good laws (good, that is, in the context of contemporary thought about penal matters) which made our prisons so shamefully bad, but the inability of Parliament to ensure that the laws it passed were carried out.

Useless though it was, the law of 1791 was until 1811 the last attempt made by the House of Commons to deal with penal problems effectively. Wars with France, which were to swallow up more of our national resources in money and labour than any previously known, and threats of invasion from across the Channel, were of more immediate importance.

Enormous efforts had been made between 1773 and 1790 to make the general public aware of the unsatisfactory nature of our gaols. The period saw much good legislation, and the efforts of John Howard, the most single-minded and energetic social reformer we have ever known. But when Howard died in 1790, after spending nearly twenty years of his life and almost his entire personal fortune in the cause of prison improvement, many prisoners were held in worse conditions than those in existence when he started his labours. The brutal practice of confinement in the Thames hulks had developed during his lifetime. These prison ships had been dreadful when they were carrying their live cargoes overseas. A third of each load had been expected to die during every journey to America. But at least the survivors had had some small hopes of a tolerable existence on arrival, with freedom ahead if they lived long enough. Since 1776 thousand upon thousand of prisoners had been in apparently perpetual confinement in verminous hulks, overcrowded and inadequately fed – rotten bread and mouldy, unsaleable ship's biscuit were their usual diet – and with nothing to hope for. At the very conclusion of his life, Howard had seen some of the survivors moved away at last, not to the penitentiaries he had worked and pleaded for, but to Australia. They had been sent off on much longer journeys than those across the Atlantic, and with a far worse prospect ahead of them than the settled colonies of America presented. Few of them expected to feel dry land beneath their feet again as the ships set sail down the Thames.

CHAPTER III

MILLBANK AND DARTMOOR

'To be therein one night its guest
'Twere better to be stoned and prest
I know none gladly there would stay,
But rather hang *out of the way. . . .'*

WILLIAM BROWNE

The year 1791 saw the publication by Jeremy Bentham, applying utilitarian principles to the problem of punishment, of *The Panopticon, or Prison Discipline.* The 'panopticon' was to be a prison constructed on entirely original principles, in such a way that the governor could keep all inmates under direct observation as he sat in a glass-walled room with separate cells ranged in a circular building around him. In such an institution, Bentham would provide useful work, from which a feeling of satisfied achievement could be gained, instead of the pointless, unfruitful tasks of hard labour which had been proposed for prisoners. This, he suggested, would teach the men to 'love labour, instead of being taught to loathe it'. His prison was to be a 'mill, for grinding rogues honest, and idle men industrious'. For a short time the architectural design put forward by Bentham for the panopticon attracted the government, and the philosopher himself purchased the Millbank site on which it could be erected.

In his struggle to fit an enlightened penal treatment which could really work into his established utilitarian principles, Bentham produced a document which combines sympathy for the prisoner, and humane methods greatly in advance of his time, with odd impracticability in detail. His thoughts having turned

> to the Penitentiary System from its first origin, and having lately contrived a Building in which any number of Persons may be kept within Reach of being Inspected during every moment of their lives, and having made out, as he flatters himself, to Demonstration, that the only eligible mode of

managing an Establishment of such a Nature in a Building of such a construction would be by Contract; [Bentham] has been induced to make public the following proposal for maintaining and employing convicts in general, or such of them as would otherwise be Confined on Board the Hulks, for twenty-five per cent. less than it costs Government to maintain them there at present; deducting also the Average Value of the Work at present performed by them for the Public; upon the Terms of receiving the Produce of their Labour.[1]

Involved in this proposal was an undertaking to:

Furnish the prisoners with a constant supply of wholesome food not limited in quantity, but adequate to each man's desires.

Keep them clothed in a state of tightness and neatness superior to what is usual even in the improved prisons.

Keep them supplied with beds and bedding competent to their situations, and in a state of cleanliness scarcely anywhere conjoined to liberty.

Ensure them a sufficient supply of artificial warmth and light.

Keep from them, in conformity with the practice so happily received, every kind of strong and spirituous liquor.

Maintain them in a state of inviolable though mitigated seclusion, in assorted companies, without any of those opportunities of promiscuous association which in other places disturb, if not destroy, whatever good effect can be expected from occasional solitude.

Give them an interest in their work by allowing them a share in the produce.

Turn the prison into a school; thereby returning its inhabitants into the world instructed in the most useful branches of vulgar learning, as well as in some trade or occupation whereby they may afterwards earn their livelihood.

Further than this, Bentham committed himself to provide work for prisoners on discharge by setting up a workshop close to the

[1] Select Committee on Police and Convict Establishments, 1798. Appendix E.

prison, where they could continue to practise the skills they had learned inside; and to establish a compulsory insurance scheme for their old age by making regular deductions from their earnings 'upon the plan of the annuity societies'. Medical treatment would be made generously available to all the prisoners during their sentences, and to assure the public that every possible care would be taken of their bodily health, he committed himself to make a standard payment for every one who died, over and above a certain fixed rate. This death rate would be based on the average for the population as a whole, and not on that for prisoners. So convinced and enthusiastic was Bentham that his scheme for the panopticon would be successful that he offered to pay the government a certain sum of money for every inmate convicted of felony after discharge, the size of the payment increasing according to the length of the stay the man had made under his care.

Such a scheme, idealistic and forward-looking though it may have been, would inevitably have failed, if only from lack of funds. Nevertheless, it was highly regarded by leading members of the Lords and the Commons when it was first published, and in 1794 a contract between Bentham and the Treasury was published, in which he undertook to build the entire establishment for only £19,000. A thousand convicts were to be housed in it, and Bentham was to receive from the Treasury a contribution of twelve pounds a year for each man in his charge. But although the sum of £2,000 was handed over to Bentham immediately, under the terms of the contract, with which to place an order for the cast-iron framework required for the panopticon, the scheme never came to fruition. The King, George III, strongly opposed the scheme, perhaps because the radical political views of Bentham displeased him; and Parliament, occupied with the threats of Napoleon, was in no mood to keep a close eye on the development of prison affairs, or to battle with the King on prison policy. It was not until 1810 that Romilly managed to arouse the attention of the House of Commons again to Bentham's scheme. Unfortunately the committee then appointed to examine the scheme once again reported unfavourably upon it. Sir Samuel Romilly and William Wilberforce joined with the other members in deciding that since the plan, excellent though it was, depended so much upon the personality of one man, for whom it might prove impossible to obtain a successor with similar qualities and ability, it could not recommend that it should be taken any further. Instead, the committee proposed that the ideas for prison construction which Howard had produced, and which had been proved in the prison erected at Gloucester in 1791, should be adopted. The committee may have been assisted, in coming to this decision, by the news that Bentham now no longer considered the original estimate of £19,000 for the cost of building the panopticon to be sufficient, and that he would demand an addition to the originally agreed £12 per head per annum as the government's payment for placing prisoners under his charge. A new Act of Parliament now placed the lands on which Bentham's mammoth institution was to have been built, in the charge of a board of three supervisors, who were to be responsible for the erection of a new penitentiary to be called Millbank.

Millbank, one of the most famous of the old London prisons, was the only national penitentiary to be erected under the provisions of the so-called 'Hard Labour Act' of Blackstone and Eden, passed in 1779. It was not until 1811, twenty-one years after Howard's death, that the building of this institution he had indirectly inspired was begun. But five years before building work began at Millbank, in 1806, another prison was being erected: Dartmoor.

Only ten years after its creation, Dartmoor was described as 'a great tomb of the living'. It was not intended as a criminal prison; it was designed for the reception of prisoners-of-war, and did not receive convicts until 1850. It is remarkable that at a time when there was such a dire need for improvement in penal matters, and the only accepted scheme for a national penitentiary was hanging fire, the government should erect, at the enormous cost of £70,000, this massive building which, if its original purpose were fulfilled, would be occupied only intermittently for short periods. Dartmoor prison was an incidental result of the architectural dreams of Sir Thomas Tyrwhitt, auditor to the Royal Duchy of Cornwall and a friend of the Prince Regent (George IV). Tyrwhitt was determined to turn the high, barren wasteland of the Moor into an extensive farming community around a model town, bringing profits to the exchequer of the Duchy. He built himself a house and laid out a farm near the present Princetown, and after several unsuccessful attempts, succeeded in growing a crop of flax in one of the less-exposed parts. But the severe climate and poor soil of the Moor made his struggles ineffective, and he died a poor man, with his greatest ambition, a flourishing community on Dartmoor, to be named Princetown in honour of the Regent, unrealized. Instead, he saw the construction of a prison there.

The Napoleonic Wars brought the problem of housing large numbers of foreign prisoners-of-war to Britain for the first time. At the beginning, the majority of the captured French were confined in Plymouth, some in a building on the shore, and some in six hulks moored outside the town: the very hulks which Howard had commented upon when he visited Plymouth in 1779. Tyrwhitt, who had the ear of the Regent, and as a Member of Parliament, first for Okehampton and later for Plymouth, had some access to the Secretary for War, first made the suggestion that these men should be moved to an inland 'depot'. Determined to prove that some human settlement on the Moor was possible, he also selected the site, than which none can ever have been more inappropriate. Prisoners had to be marched there for sixteen miles over some of the roughest country in Britain, and the climate was such that the mortality rate in the first few years after opening led to serious proposals to abandon the building so expensively constructed.

A contemporary description of Dartmoor admires it as:

. . . Probably the finest of its kind. The outer wall encloses a circle of about 30 acres. Within this is another wall which encloses the area in which the prison stands; this area is a smaller circle with a segment cut off. The prisons are five rectangular buildings *each capable of containing more than 1,500 men*; they have each two floors, where is arranged a double tier of hammocks slung on cast-iron pillars; and a third floor in the roof, which is used as a promenade in wet weather. There are besides two other spacious buildings; one of which is a large hospital and the other is appropriated to the petty officers, who are judiciously separated from the men. In the area likewise are sheds or open buildings for recreation in bad weather. The space between the walls forms a fine military road round the whole, where the guard parades, and the sentinels, being posted on the platforms, overlooking the inner wall, have complete command of the prison without intermixing with the prisoners . . . The number of prisoners that have been lodged here have been from five to seven thousand, and the troops employed to guard them not more than 300 to 500. . . .

Such a prison was far better in design than any county gaol or house of correction in England, with the exception of the model prison erected at Gloucester in 1791 on Howardian principles. If it had been erected in a more kindly part of the country, with provision for separate confinement instead of large communal wards, it would have approached the ideas of the reformers of the time. With its enormous capacity, it would have accommodated nearly half the prison population of England and Wales at the turn of the century. But its climate alone was to give it an evil reputation from the start, and when it was eventually turned into a criminal gaol it was outdated in design.[1]

There have been repeated proposals to abandon Dartmoor Prison since before the Second World War, but because of the rise in the number of men committed to prison in the last ten years, the buildings have remained in use. However, in March 1960 the Prison Commissioners produced a scheme for rebuilding the prison on a site adjoining the present one. Few penologists can fail to be aware of the undesirability of Princetown as a place for a prison where modern treatment methods are to be applied, and the reasons for the Commissioners' decision appear to be purely economic.

[1] For a full account of Dartmoor Prison, see Rhodes, A. J., *Dartmoor Prison, 1806–1932* (London, John Lane, 1933), and Thomson, B., *The Story of Dartmoor Prison* (London, Heinemann, 1907).

CHAPTER IV

AUSTRALIA DISCOVERED

*'Punishments are inflicted that crime may be prevented
and crime is prevented by reformation of the criminal.'*
THOMAS FOWELL BUXTON, 1818

Captain Cook records in his journal that when his ship
first laid anchor off the coast of New South Wales and he
took possession of the country in the name of the English
king, 'the great quantity of plants which Mr Banks and Dr
Solander collected in this place induced me to give it the name of
Botany Bay'. The first cargo of criminals to be sent to this paradise
on the resumption of transportation left the hulks at Portsmouth
in March 1787. There can hardly have been a greater contrast
than that between this collection of miserable men, herded in
nine old ships and accompanied by two men-of-war, and the
small band of idealistic Pilgrim Fathers who had crossed the
Atlantic unaccompanied so many years earlier. The first settlers
in Australia were banished from their own country, stigmatized
as criminals, with no hope of liberty before them; the passengers on
the *Mayflower* were filled with optimism, seeking freedom, and
bent upon founding a world new in its conception of human
rights and values.

There was nothing happy or pleasant about the convicts'
arrival in Australia. The rich, prolific vegetation described by
Cook could not be found: Botany Bay proved on closer examination to be an area of dank swamps and infertile sands, unfit for
human habitation; the penal settlement was started instead in a
cove jutting from the inlet which Cook had named Port Jackson.
The mean foundations of the new town were named Sydney after
the contemporary Secretary of State for the Colonies, and into
this simple clearing in an unexplored land the first party of
just over six hundred convicts were herded, under a guard of
marines.

Although thousand upon thousand of convicts were crowding

the hulks in the Thames, in the Medway, and at Portsmouth, when the first transports sailed to New South Wales, no attempt had been made to select those whose previous experience made them particularly suitable for the task of building a settlement with only natural materials at hand. If the colony were to become self-supporting; if, indeed, the new arrivals were to remain alive for more than a few months, work had to begin immediately on raising crops and building shelters. But hardly any of the convicts had had experience of farming, and few were skilled in building. Moreover, insufficient guards had been provided for the prisoners, and it was almost impossible to get them to work, unfitted as they were for the tasks now set them. Furthermore, many convicts were suffering from scurvy and other diseases generated during the eight-month voyage in cramped conditions, and there were no medical supplies with which to treat them. Forty had died during the journey; six months after embarkation, a further twenty-eight were dead, and nearly three hundred were unfit for any kind of work because of illness. Thus the labour force, originally fixed at just over six hundred, was reduced to little more than two hundred. Nevertheless, as the stores they had brought with them began to run out, a farm was started near Sydney.

The governor of the unfortunate colony, Captain Arthur Phillip, had perhaps more difficulties to cope with than the administrator of any British penal institution before or since his time. He foresaw starvation for himself, his officers and the prisoners a short time ahead; there was no proper accommodation, the convicts were unrestrained in their refusal to obey orders, and the settlement was repeatedly attacked by hostile natives. 'It soon became plain that to look for the growth of a virtuous community, except at some remote period, from the strange elements gathered together in New South Wales, was but a visionary's dream. . . .' Ironically enough, following a raid by the prisoners on the food stores, Phillip deemed it necessary to banish even from this settlement four of his colony of banished men. Only one person, apart from the governor himself, proved competent to manage the convicts and secure obedience from them: Phillip's own valet. Hardly any could be relied upon when free from the immediate supervision of one of these two men. '. . . the convicts by no means exerted themselves to the utmost;

they foolishly conceived that they had no interest in the success of their labours. . . .'[1]

Towards the end of 1789 food supplies began to run out seriously in New South Wales, and by the second month in 1790 only two months' provisions for all the inhabitants remained. Capital punishment and floggings were ordered more and more frequently as the convicts took increasingly to robbing the stores and the miserable gardens which had been established, in order to augment the rations of 2 lb. of meat, 2 lb. of rice and 2½ lb. of flour per head per week which the governor had been forced to introduce. Partly to ease this situation, Phillip ordered a number of the prisoners away to Norfolk Island, where a plentiful supply of wild birds could be shot and eaten, but on the way there the only ship left in the colony was wrecked off shore, thus severing all contact with civilization. Laing tells us in his *History of New South Wales* that 'more mouths arrived, at the time of greatest need, instead of more barrels of pork and flour'. Two hundred and twenty women convicts were delivered to add to the problem in June, 'a cargo unnecessary and unprofitable', while their escorting ship, which carried all the stores, was lost on the way. But a fleet of eleven ships, carrying food as well as further prisoners, arrived a fortnight later.

An even heavier death-rate had been suffered in this convoy on the way to Australia than in the first, and not entirely fortuitously. The transport contractors has been paid over seventeen pounds for each man and woman embarked in England.

> The more, therefore, that died, and the sooner, the less food was consumed, and the greater the profit . . . the rations were so much reduced below the level stipulated for by the governor, that many convicts were actually starved to death. What added to the horror of such a circumstance was that their deaths were concealed, for the purpose of sharing their allowance of provisions, until chance and the offensiveness of a corpse directed the surgeon, or someone who had authority in the ship, to the spot where it lay.[2]

The colony was brought to the verge of starvation again and again in subsequent years, and its population suffered poor health

[1] Gibb, Eric, *Incidents of the Convict System in Australasia* (London, 1895).
[2] Laing, op. cit.

and a high death-rate constantly, not as a result of the climate but because all the prisoners had been subjected to such appalling conditions on the way out that the hard work their officers attempted to make them do, and the salty, insufficient diet they were given, never allowed them to recover. If the convicts had been sent to Australia under better conditions in the ships; if they had been selected according to their abilities to develop a flourishing community out of a wild, uncultivated land, and given a definite promise of freedom on territory of their own, transportation might have been a human experiment in penology offering every stimulus to reform. But under these conditions it was for many of them a long-drawn-out process of execution, and for the others an equally-drawn-out torture of starvation. It was not until 1840, when Alexander Maconochie became governor of one of the Australian settlements, that the scheme produced a useful contribution to reformative methods of treating prisoners.

Phillip, looking forward, saw that the great land mass of Australia could not be colonized effectively solely by means of captive labour. Once the basic services has been provided – store-houses built, wharves made, and some farms established to pro-duce local food supplies – it would be necessary to encourage private settlers.

> People of this kind were wanted to give strength and stability to the settlement, to set an example of decorum, and by their enterprising industry to assist in the development of the country . . . they were not to be looked for among discharged soldiers, shipwrecked mariners and quondam convicts.

Therefore the governor pressed the government in England to stimulate emigration. But it was unlikely that many families would sink their capital into a voyage half-way round the world, to find at the end only a crudely developed and tiny colony, without proven prospects of wealth, populated almost entirely by criminal outlaws. A small trickle of assisted emigrants, their fares paid at public expense, arrived from 1796 onward, but well into the nine-teenth century 'a large proportion of the free settlers are des-cribed as of a low character, not very superior to that of the convicts. . . .' And alongside their small numbers, great flows of convicts kept pouring in. From 1801 until 1811, 2,398 arrived from the English hulks. The great majority were still employed in large gangs under military guard, sometimes with one of their number as an overseer, and when General Macquarie took over the governorship in 1809, less than one-eighth of the prisoners were employed privately by settlers, as agricultural labourers or personal servants, although the only payment required for them was the cost of the food they ate.

Transportation was not regarded as a positive method of building up an embryo colony into a prosperous community; indeed, the only value of the Australian territories recognized by the Crown at this time was as an easy answer to the increasing problem presented by prison conditions at home. Unable or unwilling to deal with convicts in England, the government attempted to put them out of sight on the other side of the world. The treatment was punishment in that the unfortunate men and women concerned were made an object of personal profit to the contracting firms, and subjected to the utmost economy in accommodation, food, clothing and medical care on the voyage, and that on arrival they had seven or fourteen years in the charge of unsympathetic guards before they regained liberty. In no respect could it be considered reformative, since immorality, drunkenness and crime were rampant all around them among the free settlers they would eventually join.

> The whole community might be classed into those who sold spirits and those who drank them ... there was neither marry-ing nor giving in marriage ... two-thirds of the births were illegitimate. Bands of robbers ... infested the country, levying black-mail, and entering the homes of the defenceless settlers in open day, committed the most fearful atrocities. ...

Nevertheless, at home in England, in an England disrupted during and in the years immediately after the struggle against Napoleon by economic disorder and large-scale unemployment, the fight to reform prisons and establish some ordered scheme, capable of reforming and not merely punishing offenders, flickered on. At a time when Jane Austen in her isolated social world at Chawton, was writing delicate novels, which would preserve the grace and sensibility of the early nineteenth century, Thomas Fowell Buxton produced an analysis of the life endured by prisoners. The *Inquiry whether Crime and Misery are Produced or*

Prevented by our Present System of Prison Discipline[1] was illustrated, like the work of Howard, by accounts of the author's own visits to prisons, among them to the new penitentiary at Millbank. In 1816 Buxton, an ardent speaker for prison reform in the House of Commons, had founded the *Society for the Reformation of Prison Discipline*. His *Inquiry* argued rationally about the purpose of imprisonment, and sought to find the advantages, to the State and to the individual inmate, of the present form of treatment or of any more enlightened methods which might be employed. He is thorough and complete in his condemnation of the prisons of his day.

... by the greatest possible degree of misery, you produce the greatest possible degree of wickedness ... receiving [a man] because he is too bad for society, you return him to the world impaired in health, debased in intellect, and corrupted in principles. ... It is evident, I conceive, that where the law condemns a man to jail, and is silent as to his treatment there, it intends merely that he should be amerced of his freedom, *not that he should be subjected to any useless severities.* This is the whole of his sentence, and ought therefore to be the whole of his suffering. If anyone should be disposed to hesitate in the adoption of this opinion, and should still cling to the idea, that prisons ought to be, not merely places of restraint, but of restraint coupled with deep and intense misery; let him consider the injustice, and irresistible difficulties which would result from such a system. If misery is to be inflicted at all in prisons, it ought surely to be inflicted with some proportion to the crime of the offender ; for no one could desire to visit very different degrees of guilt with the same measure of punishment. ... In fact, prisons must always, certainly under our present modes of policy they must, contain masses of offenders, with very different shades and distinctions of guilt; and we must either make imprisonment as bitter as possible, and thus involve the comparatively innocent, in those hardships which we impose upon delinquency of the deepest hue, confounding all notions of equity; or we must come to the conclusion that imprisonment is nothing more than privation of liberty, and ought therefore to be attended with as little of what is vexatious, and as little of what is hurtful as possible.

[1] London, 1818.

In its barest essence, Buxton's thesis is that men go to prison as a punishment, and not *for* punishment. If we add to this principle his proposal that punishments are inflicted to prevent crime, and that reformation of the criminal is the way to prevent crime, we have a simple philosophy of imprisonment which we can claim has been practically employed in this country only since the appointment of Alexander Paterson as a Prison Commissioner in 1921. The idea was expressed considerably in advance of the time when it could be generally accepted. We can reasonably doubt whether it is fully accepted by the British public today. Having taken it as our guiding principle in prison administration now, we still seek an answer to the complex problem it presents: how can a criminal be reformed? Sir Lionel Fox, now Chairman of the Prison Commissioners, says:

> Reform is not some specific which can be prescribed either from the prayer-book or the pharmacopoeia. It must come from something inside the man. All the prison can do is to provide the sort of conditions in which that something can be reached by the right personal influences, for this is of all things one for a rather delicate and practised personal approach. Some will be reached by the message of the Gospel, others by a friendly hint, a sympathetic touch. For one it may be necessary to prick a bladder of self-conceit, for another, carefully and patiently to build or rebuild his self-respect. . . . There are many whose rehabilitation can be effected by the removal of some mental disability by psychiatric treatment, or of some physical defect by surgery. Indeed the subtlety of variety may almost equal the number of individuals concerned.[1]

Buxton's was a reasoned approach, the approach of a theorist arguing for better conditions in the future, while concerned for the welfare of the prisoners of his own day. It was Elizabeth Fry, working at the same time, from whom came more practical and immediate sympathy.

[1] Fox, Sir Lionel, *The English Prison and Borstal Systems* (London, Routledge & Kegan Paul Ltd., 1952).

CHAPTER V

CHRISTIAN PIONEERS

There had been a prison at Newgate, in the shadow of St Paul's Cathedral, ever since the reign of King John. More men and women of fame in the history of England, William Penn and Daniel Defoe among them, have been incarcerated on this spot than at any other except Tower Hill. When Howard made his first visit there he found Richard Akerman, the friend of Boswell, as its keeper. 'The prison was dirty, the prisoners idle and dissolute. The terrible gaol fever was never long absent from its yards and cells.'

Boswell has described how a fire broke out in the officers' accommodation at Newgate, alarming the prisoners, who rushed to the gate, shouting, 'Down with it! We shall be burnt!' They were about to force the great wooden doors when Akerman appeared, quietened the mob, and told them that while under his care none of them would be allowed to escape, that the prison itself was entirely built of stone, so there could be no danger. He then promised that if they would behave themselves quietly, he would go with them, and stay with them until the flames had subsided, to prove that they need not be afraid. Once inside, Akerman ordered the gate-keeper not to open the gate, even if the inmates should force him to command it.

> Having shown them in this manner that he would die with them rather than allow a general escape, he conducted them by passages, of which he carried the keys, to a part of the gaol farthest from that where the fire was raging; and having brought them to a place of safety, addressed them. 'Gentlemen,' he said, 'you are now convinced that I told you true. I have no doubt the engines will soon extinguish this fire; if they do not, a guard will come, and you shall all be taken out. . . . I assure you, upon my word and honour, that I have not a farthing insured. I have left my house that I might take care of you. I will keep my promise, and stay with you, if you

Interior of the Panopticon Prison at Breda, erected 1901

insist upon it; but if you will allow me to go and look after my family and property, I shall be much obliged to you.' This appeal went home, and they all cried out for him to go. Happily, no further mischief was done by this fire.[1]

If there is much truth in this story, it marks out the author's friend as an extremely brave man. But courageous though he may have been, his prison was no better in administration than any other in the kingdom. It had no sanitation, the sexes were intermixed, and there was no regular work for the prisoners to do. The prison had, in fact, been condemned by the Corporation of London, and plans for a new one prepared even before Howard made his report upon it. Unfortunately, these plans could not have incorporated any of the reformer's suggestions on prison design. George Dance made a building 'of imposing majesty', 'one of the half-dozen buildings in this wilderness of bricks and mortar which have a character'.[2] The building was only partially completed in 1780, and partly occupied, when the Gordon Riots, a Protestant demonstration against the relaxation of the penal laws for Roman Catholics, broke out. Newgate was stormed and set on fire. Johnson[3] described the scene afterwards:

> . . . I walked with Dr Scott to look at Newgate, and found it in ruins, and the fire yet glowing. As I went by, the Protestants were plundering the sessions-house at the Old Bailey. There were not, I believe, a hundred; but they did their work at leisure, in full security, without sentinels, without trepidation, as men lawfully employed in full day.

Prisoners were released by the rioters, but many, having nowhere to go, and nothing to eat, hung about in the street nearby:

> . . . some famished wretch whose theft had been a loaf of bread, or scrap of butcher's meat, came skulking past, barefooted – going slowly away because that jail, his house, was burning; not because he had any other, or had friends to meet, or old haunts to revisit, or any liberty to gain, but liberty to starve and die. And then a knot of highwaymen went trooping by, conducted by the friends they had among the crowd,

---

[1] Dixon, H., *The London Prisons* (London, Jackson and Walford, 1850).
[2] Dixon, H., op. cit.
[3] *Letters to Mrs Thrale.*

D

who muffled their fetters as they went along, with handker-
chiefs and bands of hay, and wrapped them in coats and
cloaks, and gave them drink from bottles, and held it to their
lips, because of their handcuffs, which there was no time to
remove.[1]

The building was finally completed in 1785, but despite its
attractive external appearance, inside it had almost the same
design as the old one: large, communal wards in which young
and old prisoners were housed together. But some attempt was
made, in the face of the quickly increasing population of London,
and the growing number of indictable offences created by a
government full of fear, for the separation of women from men.
The inmates housed in Newgate were always more than the
building had been expected to contain. According to Neild[2] there
were 300 debtors and 900 criminals at Newgate during his visit
there. The debtors' side was originally intended for only 100
prisoners. In theory, men awaiting trial were kept separate from
others, so that new-comers were not depraved by experienced
criminals; there was a further division in which the more serious
offenders and those awaiting transportation were held. A visitor
to the prison in 1817 told his readers that children between the
ages of 8 and 12 were often to be found with them.

From 1784 Newgate became the main place of execution in
London, succeeding Tyburn. One reason for the change may have
been to give the public better facilities for observing these
spectacles, which at Tyburn had attracted dense crowds with a
fair and other sideshows giving a holiday atmosphere. It was
not until 1868 that public executions were abolished. Until
March 1957 executions carried out inside British prisons were
followed by the posting-up of a proclamation announcing the
deed at the gates.

It was in the women's wards at the new Newgate that conditions were at their worst, and it was there that the compassionate

[1] Dickens, *Barnaby Rudge.*
[2] Neild, J., *State of Prisons in England, Scotland and Wales* (London, 1812).
James Neild (1744–1814) closely modelled his career on that of John
Howard. He became Justice of the Peace in three counties, and High Sheriff of
Buckinghamshire. From 1762 he took a particular interest in the welfare of
debtors, and then retired from his prosperous business to spend twelve years
visiting more than 350 prisons in Britain, in order to describe their buildings
and administrative methods.

Elizabeth Fry began her work for prisoners. An American Quaker, Stephen Grellet, came to London in the winter of 1812 after touring the battlefields of the Napoleonic Wars. On his way he had visited many prisons, and on arriving in England he quickly found his way to Newgate. The degradation suffered by inmates there was far worse than any he had seen in continental institutions, and having accepted the hospitality of Mrs Fry during his stay in London, he lost no time in telling her of the horrors the city contained. He was particularly concerned about the viciousness of the women of Newgate.

> There were several children born in the prison among them, almost naked . . . They occupied two long rooms, where they slept in three tiers, some on the floor, and two tiers of hammocks over one another. When I first entered, the foulness of the air was almost insupportable, and everything that is base and depraved was so strongly depicted on the faces of the women, who stood crowded before me with looks of effrontery, boldness and wantonness of expression that for a while my soul was greatly dismayed.[1]

Elizabeth Fry, although now chiefly known for her activities with prisoners, had already achieved modest fame as a philanthropist and social pioneer when Grellet first appealed to her for help in alleviating the conditions of Newgate. She was born in Earlham in Norfolk of a Quaker family, the Gurneys, in 1780, and in 1800 she married another member of the Society of Friends, Joseph Fry, eventually bearing him eleven children. Her philanthropic activities were carried on while she was mistress of his houses in London and at Plashet in Suffolk, and hostess to a constant stream of English and foreign visitors. At Plashet she opened and ran a school for the children of the village and organized a voluntary society of nurses for the sick of the district. Before she died in 1845 she had also started one of the first nurses' training schools in London. This energetic and devoted woman responded immediately to Grellet's appeal. On an icy morning in January 1813, she collected what clothing she could for the inmates, and with her friend Anna Buxton entered Newgate for the first time.

The sounds which echoed down the vaulted passages and

[1] Seebohm, B., *Memoirs of the Life of Stephen Grellet* (London, 1860).

grew louder as she approached were hardly human. And when Elizabeth and her companion, following their guide, passed the barred gateway of the women's yard, they were forced to stand and look. The women, seeing visitors, pressed to the bars, stretching out greedy hands, whining, begging for pence to spend in drink at the tap of the prison. Those in front were fought with by those behind; hands snatched them back by the hair, pinched them, punched them in the ribs with fists and elbows. Elizabeth's wide eyes missed nothing. She had seen drunken Irish, gypsies in the extremes of poverty, the squalor of the London slums, but she had never seen before a mass of women, by the hundreds, reduced to the level of wild beasts.[1]

The women slept on the stone floors, without bedding; many were drunk, and all were nearly starving. It appeared that no attempt had ever been made to clean the ward in which they lived, since the day when it had been built. The keeper himself kept away from this division of the prison, and tried hard to dissuade Mrs Fry from going into it.

Within a few hours, the two women had dressed all the babies in clothes they had brought with them, and purchased clean straw for the sick to lie upon. This first visit was followed immediately by two others, when clothing was brought for the women, the ill were comforted, and hot soup was provided for all. But Elizabeth Fry was a married woman. She already had nine children to look after and she could not leave her private concerns immediately the call for aid to prisoners had been heard, as John Howard had done. It was nearly four years before she was able to return to Newgate again. At Christmas in 1816 she was able to start with her friends 'a beneficent crusade' in the prison, bringing food, clothing, 'cheerful employment' and religious ministrations to the women. In return she expected 'a voluntary subordination to the rule of sobriety, cleanliness and decent conversation'.

With the help of a Ladies' Prison Committee set up among prominent Quakers, Mrs Fry organized regular visits to Newgate and started a school for the children of the prison. As a result of the personal efforts made by these remarkably brave, self-

[1] Whitney, J., *Elizabeth Fry: Quaker Heroine* (London, Harrap & Co., 1937).

sacrificing women, the inmates' behaviour definitely improved. They received hope, sympathy and understanding as well as material help. Newgate, the 'hell above ground', became a quiet, clean and sanitary place where religious feeling was expressed without shame or self-consciousness.

Elizabeth Fry did not write a book about her experiences, or speak about them outside that circle of close friends whom she tried to persuade to help her, but her fame spread widely and she visited other prisons, including the hulks on the Thames, to repeat in them the work she had done at Newgate. In 1818 she was called before a Committee of the House of Commons to give evidence on penal conditions in the light of her experiences. The silence and devotion with which her readings of the Bible in London prisons were received, were regarded as the miracle of the age, and when, in 1821, she made a tour of provincial prisons, holding a prayer meeting in each one, she was attended by a large crowd on entering and leaving the gates. Before she died Mrs Fry visited prisons in many countries abroad, as John Howard had done before her, but making an even more remarkable impression upon their administrators by virtue of her sex.

Elizabeth Fry brought comfort to the prisoners of her day by constant devotion to them; by the natural expression of a genuine sympathy, not by theorizing or demanding political action. Hers was a reformative approach not consciously taken up as a rational one, but spontaneously forthcoming from the heart; she was too busy repairing the damage to human mind and body in prisons, and so truly Christian that she never accorded guilt or blame. Instinctively, she applied in practice the principle of her brother-in-law, Fowell Buxton, that once a prisoner is taken into captivity the task is to reform him, not to add further discomforts to the punishment of losing his liberty.

Neild, Fowell Buxton and Elizabeth Fry were not typical of their time. The majority of men and women gave no thought to the sufferings of the imprisoned, or, if they heard about them, dismissed them either as inevitable or as desirable. When Sidney Smith wrote, 'Prisons are really meant to keep the multitude in order, and to be a terror to evil doers, providing coarse food, a dress of shame; hard, incessant, irksome eternal labour; a planned and regulated and unrelenting exclusion of happiness and comfort', he was expressing the views of the majority.

Elizabeth Fry's story had elements of romance. The wealthy, well-connected woman who leaves the comfort of her home to go into the stench of a dungeon to associate with vicious women, risking personal attack and exposing herself to disease in order to serve them, is a striking heroine. But another woman was working just as devotedly for prisoners against even greater personal difficulties at the same time. Little is known of Sarah Martin, who was born in Great Yarmouth in 1791, and devoted her life from the age of nineteen until she died in 1843 entirely to the prisoners of Yarmouth Gaol. At the age of fourteen, an orphan, she left school to be trained as a dressmaker, and immediately came under the influence of a pious Nonconformist grandmother. She first entered the prison to visit a woman of her grandmother's acquaintance who had been sent there for ill-treating her child, and at once developed a powerful sympathy for all the inmates, men as well as women.

Sarah Martin's account of Yarmouth Prison when she first entered it, might well have come from the lips of Elizabeth Fry describing Newgate. She found it 'filthy, confined, unhealthy, and its occupants . . . infested with vermin and skin disease'. The inmates ranged from nine to eighty years old. All were housed together, and all were in complete idleness. Sarah's training as a dressmaker was immediately turned to good account. She collected pieces of discarded material from her friends (to whom she refused to describe conditions in the prison, for fear they would not admit her to their houses again if she did) and instructed the women in sewing clothes, the men in making straw hats and carving spoons and other useful articles from old meat-bones. Wisely, she kept the work a privilege and made idleness a punishment. The articles produced in the prison were sold, and the money thus obtained was held for the workers to be given to them on release. A small proportion was deducted for purchasing devotional books.

Sarah Martin sat up until midnight compiling accounts and records of the work done in the prison, including details of the exact verses from the Bible she gave each inmate to learn daily.

Any who could not read I encouraged to learn [she wrote]; whilst such as could write already copied extracts from books lent to them. Prisoners who were able to read, committed verses from the Holy Scriptures to memory every day, according to their ability and inclination. I, as an example, also committed a few verses to memory to repeat to them every day, and the effect was remarkable; always silencing some excuse when the pride of the prisoners would have prevented their doing it. Many said at first, 'It was no use;' and my reply was, 'It is of use to me, and why should it not be of use to you? You have not tried it, but I have.' Tracts and children's books, and larger books, four or five in number, of which they were very fond, were exchanged in every room daily; whilst any who could read more were supplied with larger books . . . and if I left home for a day or two, yet learned all the same, and most of them more, in my absence, with a view of giving me pleasure on my return.[1]

Among other records, Sarah Martin kept a *Prison Journal*, giving full details of the men and women she dealt with: their names, their religion, their status as prisoners (i.e. whether awaiting trial or convicted) and their educational standard, together with her own 'General Observations' upon their character:

Richard Conman, 23; Ranter; Felony, 6 months. *Education:* None. On leaving could read well. *Brief remarks after departure:* Temper frank and open. Attentive, answering well. Diligent, obedient. Not a corrupting one.

Many who work in prisons today will find comments on a final chat with one of her prisoners before his release appropriate even now:

I always find the worst of convicts thoughtful before their departure, and softened. The most inaccessible minds then become accessible. Such was the case with those who departed today; and, as usual, this fresh state of feeling, which was produced and prevailed before they left the prison walls, was at an end when they appeared in the street. It was then subverted by the herd around them, exciting them to laugh and shout. These were their former companions, the thieves of the place. . . .

On the 22nd of November 1832 Sarah Martin records a visit to

[1] *Sarah Martin, The Prison Visitor of Great Yarmouth: The Story of a Useful Life* (London, The Religious Tract Society, 1872).

Yarmouth Prison by Elizabeth Fry, who 'expressed her entire approbation of the cleanliness of the prisons and in every respect the regular order of the prisoners'.[1]

As well as teaching the prisoners to read, to write, and to make articles for sale, Sarah Martin acted as chaplain to them. We have an account of one of her services, written in 1835:

> The male prisoners only were assembled; a female, resident in the town, officiated; her voice was exceedingly melodious, her delivery emphatic, and her enunciation extremely distinct. The service was the Liturgy of the Church of England: two psalms were sung by the whole of the prisoners, and extremely well – much better than I have frequently heard in our best appointed churches. A written discourse of her own composition was read by her – admirably suited to the hearers. During the performance of the service the prisoners paid the most profound attention and the most marked respect, and, as far as it is possible to judge, appeared to take a devout interest.[2]

Sarah Martin was a poor woman: from the age of fourteen she kept herself entirely by dressmaking, and she could pay visits to the prison only on one day a week (the money she would otherwise have earned during that day being paid by a local philanthropist) until on her grandmother's death she received a legacy of £200. From then onward she visited the prison daily. It was only in 1841, two years before her own death, that she was persuaded to take a salary of £12 per year from Yarmouth Corporation for her prison work. She was the most truly selfless woman in the history of British social work, and is still one of the least acknowledged. Frances Banks[3] sums up the devoted career of Sarah Martin admirably:

> Truly her life was a witness, in days which we regard as cruder than our own, of the truth that there is no problem

---

[1] *Sarah Martin, The Prison Visitor of Great Yarmouth.* A brief modern account of Sarah Martin's work is given in *Sarah Martin, 1791-1843, The Prisoner's Friend,* published by the Howard League for Penal Reform.

[2] From the Report of the District Inspector of Prisons. Prison inspectors were first appointed in 1835 (see page 59). Yarmouth was one of the first institutions to be visited by them.

[3] *Teach them to Live* (London, Max Parrish, 1958).

which love – humble, firm, and as practical in detail as it was spiritual in principle – cannot solve without coercion.

The most original aspects of Sarah Martin's work, her attention to the life of prisoners after discharge and her scheme not only for arranging work in the prison but for providing inmates with some money when they left with which to make a new beginning, were not continued after her death. Towards the end of her life, Elizabeth Fry had organized a more impressive society for the care of discharged women prisoners, the aims of which were to encourage them to emigrate or to find suitable employment for them in this country. But that, too, although it had more chance of attracting official interest and was, no doubt, stronger financially than Sarah Martin's scheme, failed in a few years. Little is known of other prisoners' aid societies of this period, which were all of purely local character. That they existed spasmodically in a few places there can be no doubt, and it is clear that Elizabeth Fry's fame was responsible for stirring up the interest which created them. But until 1862, when Parliament recognized the organizations then in existence, we have little information about their work. It was not until 1955 that the Prison Commissioners began to appoint social workers to prison staffs to prepare after-care plans for individual inmates before they were discharged. They are still pitifully few in number, and the most common tendency is still to use the services of already grossly overworked local probation officers to help long-term prisoners on their return home.

CHAPTER VI

THE NATIONAL
PENITENTIARY

The great national penitentiary at Millbank was finally completed in 1821, at a total cost of over £500,000.[1] It was one of the most expensive buildings ever erected in Britain at that time, a large proportion of the money having been wasted: the soft, marshy earth swallowed up thousands of pounds, as repeated attempts were made to establish firm foundations in it; a firmer and equally satisfactory site could have been found just as near London. The influence of Bentham's panopticon was strong:

'The Penitentiary', as it is still commonly called, looks on London maps like a six-pointed star-fort; built, say, against catapults and old-fashioned engines of war. The central point is the chapel, a circular building which, with the open space around it, covers more than half an acre of ground. A narrow building, three storeys high, and forming a hexagon, surrounds the chapel, with which it is connected at three points by covered passages. This chapel and its annular belt, the hexagon, forms the omphalos of the whole system. It is the centre of the circle, from which the several bastions of the star-fort radiate. Each of these salients is in shape a pentagon, and there are six of them, one opposite each side of the hexagon. They are built three storeys high, on four sides of the pentagon, having a small tower at each external angle; while on the fifth side a wall about nine feet high runs parallel to the adjacent hexagon. In these pentagons are the prisoners' cells, while the inner space in each, in area about two-thirds of an acre, contains the airing yards, grouped round a tall central watchtower. The ends of the pentagons join the hexagon at certain points called junctions. The whole space covered by

---

[1] Holford, G. P., *An Account of the General Penitentiary at Millbank* (London, 1828).

these buildings has been estimated at about seven acres, and something more than that amount is included between them and the boundary wall, which takes the shape of an octagon, and beyond which was a moat, now filled up. . . .

There was one old warder who served for years at Millbank, and rose through all the grades to a position of trust, who was yet unable, to the last, to find his way about the premises. He carried with him a piece of chalk, with which he 'blazed' his path as the American backwoodsman does the forest trees. Angles every twenty yards, winding staircases, dark passages, innumerable doors and gates – all these bewilder the stranger, and contrast sharply with the extreme simplicity of modern prison architecture.[1]

In February 1816 it was announced that the first pentagon was ready to receive prisoners, and the Prince Regent, in residence at the Royal Pavilion in Brighton, nominated a committee of twenty, including the Speaker of the House of Commons, to superintend its management. The first batch of prisoners, thirty-six women transferred from Newgate, arrived on 27 June, and it was expected that by the end of 1816 two of the pentagons would be fully occupied. But 'in September . . . alarming symptoms of failure and settlement appeared in the building. Serious cracks and fissures opened in the walls of Pentagon No. 1, and the safety of the whole edifice was for the moment in question.' There followed a further demand for money from Parliament, while the foundations were examined once more and reconstruction of a great deal of the still incomplete building took place. It was not until 1817 that the second pentagon was occupied. When, in 1821, the prison was finished, it had accommodation for a thousand convicts, men and women.

Millbank was the first prison to which appointments of Governor, Medical Officer, Chaplain, Master Manufacturer and Lady Matron were made from the very start. This very fact is a tribute to the way in which the ideas of Howard, Elizabeth Fry and Fowell Buxton had to some degree influenced Parliament. But none of the gentlemen appears to have been entirely suitable for his office. John Shearman, the first governor, was second clerk at the police offices in Hatton Garden. He resigned shortly

[1] Griffiths, A., *Memorials of Millbank* (Chapman & Hall, 1884).

after his appointment at Millbank because the Committee objected to his frequent absences from the penitentiary in order to
carry on a private practice as a solicitor. The Bishop of London,
writing to recommend Samuel Bennett as first chaplain, stressed
this candidate's financial need rather than any interest he may have
had in taking part in a great reformative experiment: '. . . I think

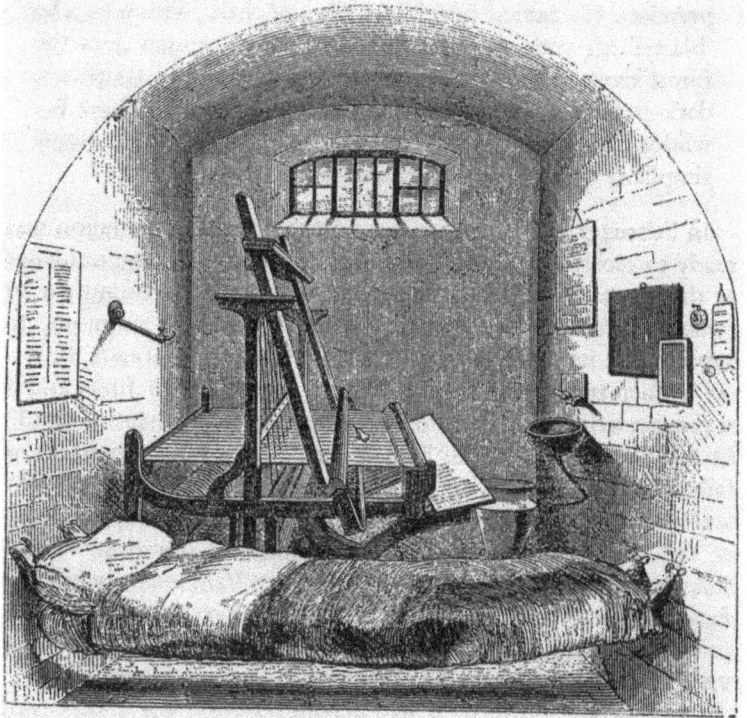

Pentonville Prison, *c.* 1850
Inmates worked alone at looms in their cells. The hammock
was removed during the day

he will not refuse, as he finds the income of his curacy inadequate
to the maintenance of a family, and is precluded from residence
on a small property by want of a house and the unhealthiness of
the situation.' A Mr Webbe was made master manufacturer,
merely, it seems, because he was of a 'mechanical turn of mind,
he had made several articles of workmanship, and he produced
to the committee specimens of his shoemaking . . .' Of Webbe's

administrative and managerial abilities, the committee did not appear to require evidence. But in considering the appointment of a matron, the committee looked for qualities similar to those which might be sought in a Borstal matron today. The woman selected 'has much firmness of character, with a compassionate heart, and I am firmly persuaded will most conscientiously perform every duty she undertakes to the utmost of her power and ability'. Elizabeth Fry had proposed the appointment of a matron in each prison, instinctively realizing what a valuable influence a sympathetic woman of good education and strong personality could have. In 1816, it had been believed by many of the superintendents of Millbank that it would be impossible to

> procure any person of credit or character to undertake the duties of a situation so arduous and so unpleasant . . . How difficult it must be to find a female educated as, and having the feelings of, a gentlewoman, who would undertake a duty so revolting to every feeling she has hitherto possessed, and even so, alarming to a person of that sex.

The practice of appointing matrons in prisons is not continued today, but few who have experience of the Borstal system would deny the value of their work among older adolescent boys. The appointment of a lady Tutor Organizer at Maidstone Prison (a men's prison) in 1951, and the immeasurable good influence she had upon the inmates there, suggests that it might not be unwise, if professional women with the same rare qualities should present themselves, to make a few responsible posts in the men's training prisons available to women in the future.[1]

The prisoners at Millbank occupied separate cells, but there was no completely solitary confinement except for men and women undergoing punishment for a breach of the regulations of the institution. On arrival, inmates were kept in accommodation at the gate for five days, without work, in order to 'awaken them to reflection and a due sense of their situation'. During this period of 'meditation' the governor would visit each one personally, to assess his character and explain to him 'the spirit in which this establishment had been erected'. Such contact between the chief administrator of a prison and his charges was in itself one

[1] See *Teach them to Live*, by Frances Banks (London, Max Parrish, 1958).

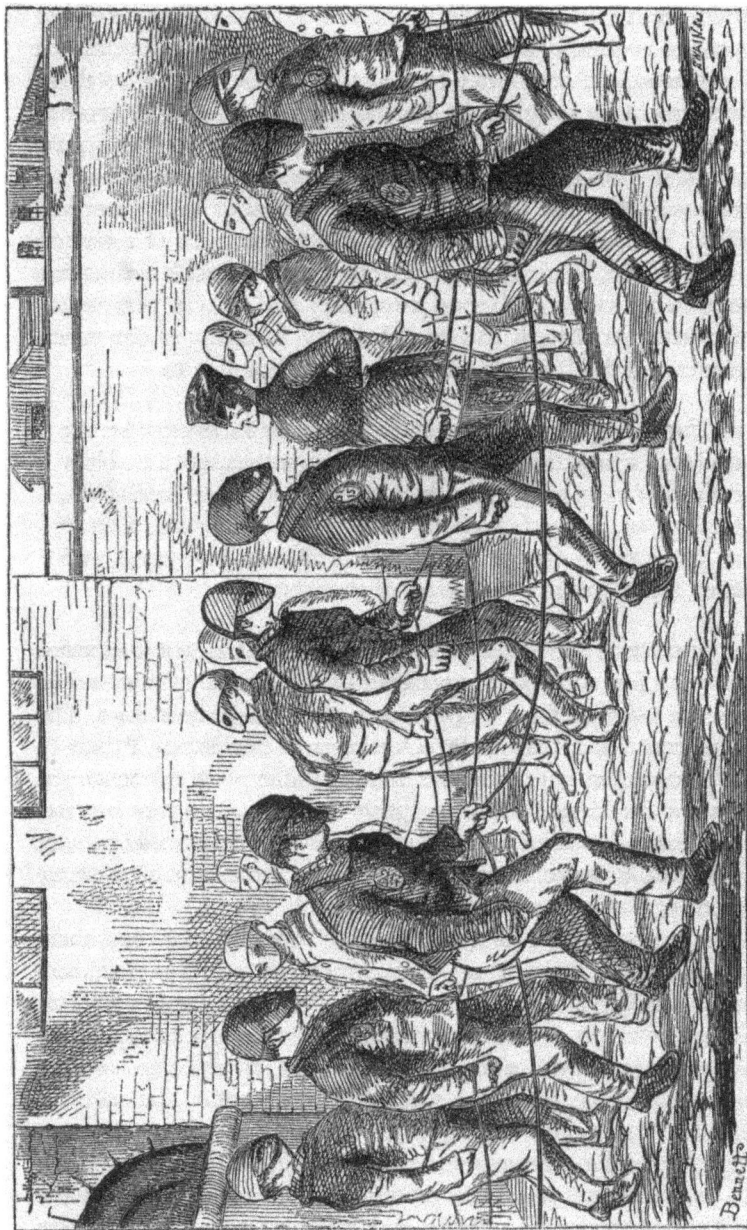

Pentonville Prison, c. 1850. Convicts exercising wore masks to prevent recognition

of the most revolutionary innovations at Millbank. After this preliminary, the prisoners entered the 'first class' of the prison, a stage lasting for half their sentences, during which they would work alone in their own cells; the 'second class', in which they came for the remainder of their time at Millbank, was spent working in association with other inmates.

Elizabeth Fry had said:

> The benefit which society enjoys from the employment of prisoners greatly outweighs the inconvenience which can possibly arise to the mass of our labouring population from the small proportion of work done in our prisons. . . . My idea with regard to . . . employment . . . is that it should be a regular thing, undertaken by Government; considering that there are so many to provide for; there is the Army and the Navy and so many things required for them; why should not Government make use of the prisoners?[1]

But in Millbank in 1821, as in the English prisons today, it was not easy to find work suitable for the prisoners to do. At first, tailoring was tried for the men, and needlework for the women, and a variety of other trades were introduced, prisoners skilled in them being called upon to impart their abilities to the others. But in 1822 we find that the committee had to admit failure in this. The skilled prisoners were not always those who could best have confidence placed in them. Their trusted positions were invariably abused for the opportunities they provided for trafficking and other forbidden practices. All manufacturing in the prison was abandoned that year, apart from shoemaking, tailoring and weaving under the direction of a member of the staff. Soon afterwards, shoemaking was objected to, since the prisoners engaged in it had to be provided with sharp, potentially dangerous implements, and the infrequency with which a good cutter was committed to the prison made it difficult to continue tailoring. Weaving was left as the only trade, among a score which had been experimented with, which could be practised at Millbank.

It is necessary here to recall how original the whole conception of a national penitentiary was. The committee had no precedents to guide them. Theirs were the first serious attempts in England to

---

[1] Whitney, op. cit.

keep prisoners fully employed in useful work during sentence, and theirs was the first penal institution from which the government expected reformative work. However well intentioned, they had to be tentative in all the work they did. Griffiths admirably sums up the situation, as it was regarded by the government of the day, by describing Millbank as 'a sort of crucible into which the criminal elements were thrown, in the hopes that they might be changed or resolved by treatment into other superior forms'. There was no definite scheme, good or bad, which the committee could take as a pattern. They had an enormous and unique building, on which the interests of all the philanthropists of the day were focused, and the majority of them were very sensible of the great opportunities they had to produce a good 'system of prison discipline'; but they could only feel their way nervously to a solution. They were pestered by frequent visits from the dignitaries and leading citizens of the day, to whom 'Millbank was a huge plaything . . . it was easy to see that they loved to run in and out of the place, and to show it off to their friends'.

The governor was remarkably gentle in treating the prisoners; punishments were few, and could not be inflicted by a warder without consulting one of his superiors. When the time came for the first prisoner to be released, a didactic little ceremony took place. Mary Turner was dressed in her 'liberty clothing', and taken round in turn to the exercise yards where the other inmates could see her, while the Visitor 'represented to them in a most impressive manner' the advantages which they could all have if they, like Mary Turner, behaved themselves at Millbank. 'The whole were most sensibly affected, and I think the event will have a very powerful effect on the conduct of many and prove an incentive to observe good will and orderly demeanour', wrote Shearman in his journal for that day. All the female prisoners clambered up to the windows and shouted good wishes to Mary Turner early next morning, when she left the gates. 'The whole place appears to have been like a big school . . .' says Griffiths with wonder.

It was optimistic of the superintendents to receive convicts from such places as a Newgate where Elizabeth Fry's efforts had not yet produced that placid, receptive atmosphere she so astonishingly achieved, and to expect them, in their hundreds, to react favourably to leniency. Many must have been puzzled and made suspicious by the gentleness with which they were now handled. Inevitably, coming from such dens of horror to an institution where the supervising committee calmly considered their petitions against even the rare punishments inflicted, they would try to find how far they could go in misbehaviour without stringent reprisals.

In April 1818 a riot broke out in Millbank, in protest against a change in the bread which was an important proportion of their diet. It was a rebellion led mainly by the female prisoners, who threw the loaves out of their doors into the passages, and later, in company with the men, punctuated the chapel service by raining bread down upon the heads of chaplain and governor. Next morning, the governor told each prisoner individually that the new bread would continue to be supplied until the committee had met to discuss the matter, 'whereupon many resisted when their cell doors were being shut, and others hammered loudly on the woodwork with their three-legged stools; and this was accompanied by the most hideous shouts and yells'.

Four prisoners, who were sharing one cell, completely destroyed the outer door, all the furniture inside, and the two windows, which were in iron frames; then they managed to dislodge pieces of stone from around the doorway, flinging them against the windows of the passage opposite. One, Greenslade by name, attacked the governor with part of the door frame when he entered to try and pacify them, but 'I parried the blow and drove the prisoner's head against the wall; and I was also compelled, in my defence, to knock down [another prisoner]'.[1] The governor was forced to call in the Bow Street runners and post them in different points throughout the building to restore order. The next day, a fresh tumult of shouting broke out when the bell rang for chapel, and the governor now took punitive action, by handcuffing all the prominent offenders. This action immediately quelled the riot, and later all the refractory men were placed in irons, until the committee met and formally administered punishment, mainly by awarding a reduction in class.

The riot considerably shook the confidence of the public in Millbank, which had appeared from outside to be managed so smoothly and successfully. In 1823 a second sensation, the outbreak of an epidemic among the prisoners, led to a Parliamentary

---

[1] *Governor's Journal, 1818.*

Enquiry into the whole question of its administration.[1] In 1822 the prisoners' health 'began visibly to decline'. They lacked energy, lost weight and appeared unable to perform the same amount of work as they had done before. Many of the women began to faint frequently. But there were no definite signs of disease until January 1823, when scurvy appeared. Unfortunately, the medical officer in charge chose to conceal the fact that he had noticed this, in order to prevent a general alarm; but by March the spongy gums and blotchy legs of many of the inmates indicated that the disease was spreading rapidly. Diarrhoea and dysentery followed, affecting over half the population, but more women than men. A change in the diet, including the provision of fresh fruit daily, checked the scurvy; but within weeks a second and more serious outbreak, this time of cholera, occurred.

By the 23rd of May 1823, 454 prisoners out of a total of 800 were affected. There were thirty deaths. It was realized that only a complete change from the confined atmosphere of the prison could give the inmates any chance of restoring their health entirely, and that only if the prison were entirely emptied of people could it be fumigated and cleansed sufficiently to ensure that it would not continue to harbour the disease. Accordingly, a special Act of Parliament was passed to enable the prisoners to be moved away from Millbank. A proportion was sent to the empty Royal Ophthalmic Hospital in Regent's Park, and the majority to a hulk at Woolwich specially prepared for the purpose. The men at Woolwich showed signs of improvement almost immediately they had arrived there, but the women, all of whom had been sent to Regent's Park, made little progress. Fresh attacks continued among them, and it seemed that the only hope of restoring their health was to set them free.[2] All the women were pardoned, and it is interesting here to note that before they were set at liberty the Home Office communicated with their friends and relatives, and no one was released until it was made certain that she had a home awaiting her. It was very many years before

[1] The governor, to whom it is difficult to accord blame directly for the riot, was dismissed by the visiting committee after its investigation into the causes of the riot, and after he had repeatedly refused to resign.

[2] It is hard to follow the medical officers' reasoning. At home the prisoners were hardly likely to receive medical attention. Moreover, by distributing so many women, suffering from a contagious disease, throughout the kingdom the doctors were taking the risk of starting a civilian epidemic.

such concern for the well-being of prisoners on discharge was again displayed in a practical way in England. In the meantime, the men's health had become almost completely restored, but they were 'lapsing into utter anarchy and confusion' on the hulk, and the government was nervous of extending a similar pardon to them. They were therefore distributed among the regular hulks, and never returned to the national penitentiary. For some months it remained vacant, and was eventually repopulated with a completely different set of prisoners.

The Parliamentary Committee enquiring into the epidemics reported favourably upon Millbank from the hygienic point of view. It could not find anything in its situation, in the design and construction of the building, 'nor in the moral and physical treatment of the prisoners confined therein, to injure health or render them peculiarly liable to disease'. Nevertheless, it ordered 'certain external and internal improvements' with the stress on better ventilation. And the ditch surrounding the prison 'dignified with the name of moat', quite probably a breeding ground for disease-carrying insects, was connected with the Thames, to be freshened by the tides. In considering the evidence of the doctors they had examined, 'who were agreed that cheerfulness and innocent recreation were conducive to health . . .', the committee proposed that the prisoners might be allowed games and sports during some part of each day. 'Fives courts and skittle alleys were probably in their minds, with cricket in the garden, or football during the winter weather . . .' The cells should be lit with candles, and more educational facilities should be provided, 'as a profitable method of employing hours otherwise lost, and breaking in on the monotony and dreariness of the long dark nights'. Additional stoves were to be provided, and the diet made more generous and nutritious.

Thus comfortably lodged [says Griffiths], and warmly clad, fed with so much wasteful luxury that daintiness soon supervened, their every want thus tenderly forestalled – the condition, but for one drawback, of these rogues, was far superior to that of soldiers or sailors, or the honest poor who had done no wrong; that drawback was the loss of liberty, yet many would have cheerfully sacrificed it for the ease and comfort of the Pentitentiary.

We can, perhaps, forgive Griffiths' imagination by remembering that he wrote (in 1884) as the national prison system of England was entering its harshest and least reformative phase. Even in the far more comfortable, and far better equipped prisons of modern times, daintiness among prisoners in the dining-halls would cause some surprise. And the many excellent men and women in the Prison Service do not even yet 'tenderly forestall' the every want, in food and amusement, of their charges.

To give the national penitentiary, in its openly reformative policy, every opportunity of success now that it was reopened, the inmates were very carefully selected: the most hopeful prisoners of both sexes were sent there, in three classes:[1]

(*a*) Young persons.

(*b*) First offenders.

(*c*) Those whose 'early habits and good character . . . afford reasonable hope of their being restored to society corrected and reclaimed by the punishment they had undergone'.

Thus Millbank started a new life in 1824, under a rudimentary scheme of prisoner classification, more full of promise than it had been in the eight years of disruption since it first received prisoners. As the first national prison in Britain for ordinary citizens who had fallen foul of the law, it was a remarkably idealistic institution, pursuing acknowledged aims not much less enlightened than those we try to achieve today. Its eventual failure was due, not to the wrong object being held in view, but to the lack of any sound scheme for carrying out that object. It failed because of method, not because of aim. And it was many years before any body of information was assembled which could lead us to a system offering a reasonable, rational hope of even partial success in doing what Millbank now attempted.

[1] Act of 4 Geo. IV., c. 64.

CHAPTER VII

TREADMILL

'The cell is, in fact, the criminal's strait-jacket. It keeps him very quiet, makes him very obedient; but the question, nevertheless, remains an open one – Does it make him a better man? What we want are sound minds, not quiet men in strait-jackets; good citizens, not submissive criminals in silent cells. . . .'

HEPWORTH DIXON, 1850

The Act of 1823, introducing the classification system at Millbank, was the first statute effecting a general reform of prisons to be enacted by Parliament. It formed part of a policy of consolidating the criminal law carried out by the most energetic of all Home Secretaries, Sir Robert Peel, who was sympathetically aware of the thinking of contemporary reformers. His work in this field indicates the immense influence an enlightened, forward-looking Secretary of State can have upon social policy, even at a time when the majority in Parliament and in the country are less advanced in their views.

Now for the first time, Justices were ordered to supply the Home Secretary with quarterly reports 'upon every department of their prison administration'. They were required to accept the major principles expressed by Howard: that the gaol keeper should be a paid servant of the local authority; that prisons should be sanitary as well as secure; that a 'reformatory régime' should be applied to all prisoners, and that every part of every prison should be systematically inspected at regular intervals. Gaolers were excluded from doing private business with their charges, and the supervision of female prisoners was placed exclusively under female warders. Use of irons, chains and 'tyrannical punishments' must be notified to the Justices in every case. But even Peel, the great administrator, who, in another field of criminal treatment, established the Metropolitan Police Force of London, failed to ensure that this excellent, forward-looking legislation would be carried into practice. The creation of an inspectorate with Parliamentary authority was not even contemplated. Furthermore, the Act applied only to the prisons under County Justices, to those in London and Westminster and in seventeen other cities and towns. It left untouched prisons in the smaller towns: the prisons which were most in need of the fresh winds of reform.

The next ten years saw Peel's Act slowly and unevenly adopted in some of the 130 prisons to which it applied. In most cases, implementation of the Act made it necessary to reconstruct buildings formerly used as prisons, and in considering the design of new ones, the Justices became involved in controversies over the advantages and disadvantages of the classification system and the 'separate system', the provision of useful work for prisoners or the introduction of hard, profitless, but degrading labour.

> What gave acrimony to the interminable controversy which now set in, was not so much the conflict of evidence as to the efficacy of the particular devices, as the unavowed differences in opinion upon the relative importance to be attached, not merely to the maintenance of the prisoners in physical and mental health, but also to success in economizing public expenditure.[1]

The overcrowding, and the intermixing of young and old, experienced criminal with novice, which had taken place in the old prisons, led Howard to insist always on both 'separation' (in solitary sleeping-cells) and 'classification' when at work or in association during the day. In the prison at Gloucester, erected on Howardian principles by Sir George Onesipherous Paul, classification had been ignored. His was a régime in which the prisoners slept and were employed individually in cells; with chapel services, and twenty minutes each day at the treadmill and at walking exercise, all in silent (i.e. with talking forbidden) association. But from 1810 onward there were protests among certain men interested in penal matters against the 'silent' system, following rumours of insanity caused by it among the prisoners at Petworth, another gaol run on these lines. These protests, feebly expressed though they may have been, were taken up by the Justices with an eagerness they had never before accorded to the utterances

[1] Webb, S. and B., op. cit.

of prison reformers, and were used in many counties as a justification for omitting separation in cells altogether, in favour of a
classified régime. The expense of building a cellular prison was
enormous. But an institution in which prisoners of the same
classification could be herded together for sleeping and working
periods, could be erected much more cheaply. The population of
England and Wales was increasing rapidly at this time, and with
the increase came a rise in the number of crimes committed.
Therefore, the pressure upon prison buildings was greater than
at any time before, just at the moment when there was a call for
demolition of the old structures in favour of new ones. In addition
to the question of expense there was speed of erection in favour
of prisons to be run on the 'classified' system. The Act of 1823
had, indeed, supported the protagonists of the 'classification'
school to the extent of abandoning rigid insistence on absolutely
separate sleeping accommodation for each prisoner; and in 1824
a further Act provided that 'where in any prison there shall be
only one prisoner belonging to any class, such prisoner may be
assigned, with his or her consent, to any other class of prisoners
of the same sex'.[1] Uncontrolled association among prisoners, even
if they were sleeping only three or four in a cell, allowed all the
possibilities of contamination which Howard and Elizabeth Fry
had protested against. The very way in which classification was
made, by considering only the crime for which the prisoners were
now being punished, increased chances of contamination. A man
might have committed serious offences, and been punished for
them, before returning to prison again on a minor charge, to
associate with a young man who had been forced by starvation
to commit a single theft. And sometimes 'the burglar was sent
to prison for trying his hand at begging, a professed sheep-stealer
for doing a little business as a thimblerig man, and a London thief
for showing fight at a country fair'.[2] Bentham's panopticon had
envisaged separation in the national penitentiary. The building
erected at Millbank on his site, already different in design and
administration from his ideal, moved still further away from it
after Peel's Act.

Millbank Prison had not been a success in providing useful
profitable work for prisoners, even in the first year after it was

[1] 5 George IV, c. 85, sec. 13.
[2] Jebb, Colonel Joshua, *Modern Prisons* (London, 1844).

fully completed. But great stress had been placed upon hard labour in the Act of Blackstone and Eden which brought into being the idea of a national penitentiary. Although it had been so long before this Act produced a building, its plea for hard, unremitting physical work for criminals had found a place in the English mind.

There were two different schools of thought upon the question of hard labour during the first third of the nineteenth century. One group proposed that it should be as tiring and pointless as possible, of such utter degradation that it would be a major deterrent to imprisonment in itself, and the other, the economizing group, saw in it an opportunity for reducing the cost of dealing with offenders by undertaking the manufacture of saleable goods. Thus we find the treadmill in use in some prisons, and other institutions which were almost like factories, with inmates hard-pressed to produce articles of some practical use. In Nottinghamshire the Justices ordered that prisoners held in the house of correction at Southwell, should be employed 'on some work or labour which is not severe' *if they were kept and maintained at the county expense*, 'though by warrant of commitment such persons are not ordered to be kept to hard labour'.[1] But it was not easy to obtain work of a profitable kind for prisoners, or to find inmates who were able to do it. Only the simplest tasks, requiring no skill, could be performed *en masse* by such a heterogeneous collection of men and women. The treadmill, on the other hand, was simple, and, as Sydney Smith wrote in praising its use, 'economical, certain, well-administered, little liable to abuse, capable of infinite division, a perpetual example before the eyes of those who want it, affecting the imagination only with horror and disgust, and affording great ease to the Government'. The Act of 1779 had, in fact, suggested the employment of prisoners, in so many words, in activity *such as treading in a wheel*, or drawing in a capstan, for turning a mill or other machine or engine. A treadmill suitable for use in prisons was designed in 1818 by William Cubitt, a Lowestoft engineer, intended for a county prison at Bury, and soon afterwards there were few prisons in which one had not been installed. Sometimes the Justices found to their satisfaction that the degrading 'everlasting staircase',

[1] House of Commons Committee on the Laws Relating to Penitentiary Houses, 1811.

inflicting its torture and tedium upon their unfortunate fellow-men, could be combined with a profit-making venture such as grinding corn or raising water. *Hansard*, on the 5th of March 1824, contains a report of the way in which the governor of Northallerton Prison hired out the labour of his charges to a local miller, as they silently, painfully, ground the treadmill round, 'like so much water power or steam'. Clay[1] tells us that it was heresy to question the reformative effect of the treadmill upon convicts:

> The only point on which there existed any difference of opinion was as to the number of diurnal revolutions which yielded a maximum of reforming power. Some magistrates kept their prisoners treading from morning to night, till they half-killed them; others were content with requiring a modicum of wholesome exercise on the wheel for three or four hours a day . . . there is so little uniformity as regards the number of hours devoted to labour, the height of the steps of the wheel, and the rapidity of its rotation, that in some prisons the punishment is nearly three times as severe as in others. . . .

The use of the treadmill was a subject of protest and justification for many years. Some claimed that it led to bodily and internal injuries to the prisoners, and many reformers claimed that it destroyed any efforts which might be made towards the improvement of inmates' characters.

Yet in, spite of all criticism, it spread from gaol to gaol, vehemently attacked by humanitarians, not only as cruel, but also as ineffective in working any reform of the convict; and no less obstinately defended by Justices in search of a punishment at once cheap and easy of application, and potent as a deterrent. . . . When exacted in sufficient quantity, this form of penal discipline certainly deterred persons from using the gaol as a convenient place of refuge in seasons of adversity. On the other hand, the weight of evidence indicates that labour on the tread-wheel was habitually injurious to the bodily health of women, and occasionally to that of men,

[1] Clay, W. L., *The Prison Chaplain* (London, 1861).

whilst it was always physically depressing, personally degrading, and unproductive either of mental initiative or
emotional regeneration.[1]

This was a period of increasing public discussion concerning
prisons. It was also a time of complete chaos in their administration and organization. The reformers did not agree among themselves: there was no single clear-cut policy of reform to press
upon the government. Instead, there was a crowd of people demanding reform but shouting different things in a babble, not
one thing in chorus. In questions of diet, religious worship,
labour, and education, the Justices went their own way, influenced, whether they were good or bad, more by emotional
generosity or by the desire to economize than by any rational
desire to help or chastise the prisoners.

It was not until 1835, following a House of Lords Committee
of investigation into the state of *all* the prisons in England and
Wales, that an Act 'for effecting greater uniformity of practice
in the government of the several prisons in England and Wales,
and for appointing inspectors of prisons in Great Britain' was passed
by a Whig government filled with reforming zeal in every sphere
of domestic politics.

[1] Webb, S. and B., op. cit.

CHAPTER VIII

A DRESS OF SHAME

'They made separation so complete that its depressing influence took all the starch out of the prisoners' characters, and rendered both their wits and their wills limp and flabby.'   W. L. CLAY

Our Convict Systems, 1862

The period of classified association produced its own distinctive fashion of prison architecture, notably at Maidstone, where the prison is to this day a series of detached blocks built round the old governor's residence in the centre.[1] The need for close central control of prisons was clear to the House of Commons Committee which met in 1832 under a government convinced that its extensive schemes for general social reform must, if they were to follow a common policy, be enforced from Westminster. But the committee reported at a time when Parliament was too preoccupied with other legislation to take any immediate action. The House of Lords Committee, which followed, and the Act of 1835, again stressed this principle. For the next forty years, until the formation of the Prison Commission 'nationalized' all the English prisons, the Justices who administered local prisons, and the corporations who supplied funds for them, were made increasingly subject to rules dictated by the Home Office. In following these rules, they were closely watched by the salaried inspectors created under the Act: the first body of professional men exclusively concerned with prison administration to come into existence in this country. Thus was ensured an ever-increasing fund of knowledge and experience relating to penal problems, which could be passed on to successors in the inspectorate. No longer were the men involved in prison organization entirely separate from one another, with no co-ordination by which methods could be passed on and either generally adopted or generally condemned.

[1] The 'Round House' described by Banks, op. cit.

59

It was now that the great argument over the relative values of the 'separate' and 'silent' systems of prison discipline arose. The Act of 1835 had already disposed of the idea of classified association, its authors being convinced of the evils of contamination which sprang from it. But it was the curiosity aroused not only in England but throughout the prison systems of Europe, by the form of separate confinement being practised in the United States of America, which eventually led to the restoration of strict separation in this country.

In the United States the use of imprisonment as a form of punishment can be given a definite date. When independence was achieved, the most common forms of punishment in America were the pillory, the whipping-post and the branding-iron. Adulteresses were still branded with the letter 'A'. The state of Pennsylvania soon replaced hangings with hard labour publicly performed: its prisoners dug drains or swept the streets in chains with heavy iron balls attached to their feet. It was in 1787 that Benjamin Rush, a prominent physician, proposed, in a paper read at a small meeting in Benjamin Franklin's home, that imprisonment should be imposed, instead of social degradation, as the penalty for crime. Work was the way to rehabilitation: criminals should be classified and segregated, and put to work in prisons where their sentences would be indeterminate and release dependent upon their progress. In 1790 a law was passed which led to the creation of the Pennsylvania prison system precisely on these lines. A block of cells was built within the grounds of the Walnut Street Gaol in Philadelphia, and it first came into use in 1792. Each of its three stories contained eight cells separated by a corridor, four feet wide, running down the centre. Each cell had two doors, held by heavy locks and bars; at the end of each corridor were two more doors; and a further door, stronger even than these, stood at the top of each staircase. Barnes and Teeters, the distinguished American criminologists, quote a contemporary description.[1]

> In every cell there is one small window, placed high up and out of reach of the convict; the window well secured by a double iron grating, so that, provided an effort to get to it was successful, the person could perceive neither heaven nor earth, on account of the thickness of the wall. The criminal, while

[1] *New Horizons in Criminology* (New York, 1943).

confined here, is permitted no convenience of bench, table, or even bed, or anything else but what is barely necessary to support life, without a risk of endangering his health. . . . No communication between the prisoners in the different cells can be effected. That the criminal may be prevented from seeing any persons as much as possible, his provisions are only brought to him once a day, and that in the morning.

The Walnut Street Gaol was quickly copied by other American states, but these institutions quickly became overcrowded, and the practice of absolute separate confinement had to be abandoned within a few years. The Pennsylvania Prison Society, of which Rush and other prominent Quakers were members, then campaigned for the erection of a new institution where the principle could be given a fair trial. As a direct result of their efforts two buildings were erected, providing basic prison designs which were copied all over the United States and western Europe in the nineteenth century. Cherry Hill (officially the Eastern Philadelphia Penitentiary) was opened in 1829. All the prisoners there were kept in solitary confinement. Inmates were put into their cells, alone with the Bible and a task of work such as shoemaking or spinning. They never associated freely with other human beings, and even took their exercise (restricted to one hour a day) in private little yards adjoining their cells. Even during religious services, no prisoner was allowed to see another or even to see the minister. Cell doors were opened and the chaplain conducted the services from one end of the intervening corridor, with a black curtain drawn down the middle of it so that inmates could hear only his voice and see nothing.

The second building, Auburn Prison in New York state, saw a different system of handling prisoners, known as the silent system. Prisoners were led out of their cells during the day to work together in a central shop, but they were forbidden to speak to one another. When moving about the prison under the watchful eye of an officer, they marched with faces cast down toward the floor. Floggings for infringement of these rules were common. Unlike the cells at Cherry Hill, each of which had a window (although inmates could never see out of it) opposite a door which led out on to the central corridor, the Auburn cells were built 'back to back' with air and light coming in from a grating in the doors.

There, the doors opened into narrow corridors which ran along each side of the cell blocks, so that the only view from the gratings was of a plain brick wall.

From 1790 to 1825 the chief controversy over prison construction was whether inmates should mix freely or be confined separately. From 1825 onward the battle was waged over the relative advantages of the Auburn system, which prevented moral contamination by silence, and the Pennsylvania system, which prevented it by an enforced solitude, giving prisoners an opportunity of introspection and repentance.

While in Britain argument continued as to whether prisons should be the concern of central or of local government, the United States, with its bright new Constitution allocating responsibility in social matters to the individual states, went ahead with large prison-building programmes, the policy of each state showing clearly its loyalty to the principles either of Cherry Hill or of Auburn. The rival American systems attracted the attention of European visitors, and Dickens commented upon the Pennsylvanian prison:

In its intention, I am well convinced that it is kind, humane, and meant for reformation; but I am persuaded that those who devised this system of Prison Discipline, and those benevolent gentlemen who carry it into execution, do not know what it is they are doing. I believe that very few men are capable of estimating the intense amount of torture and agony which this dreadful punishment, prolonged for years, inflicts upon the sufferers; and in guessing at it myself, and in reasoning from what I have seen written upon their faces, and what to my certain knowledge they feel within, I am only the more convinced that there is a depth of terrible endurance in it, which none but the sufferers themselves can fathom, and which no man has the right to inflict upon his fellow-creatures. I hold this slow and daily tampering with the mysteries of the brain, to be immeasurably worse than any torture of the body: and because its ghastly signs and tokens are not so palpable to the eye and sense of touch as scars upon the flesh; because its wounds are not upon the surface, and it extorts few cries that human ears can hear; therefore I the more denounce it, as a secret punishment which slumbering humanity is not roused up to stay. I hesitated once, debating with myself, whether, if I had the power of saying 'Yes' or 'No', I would allow it to be tried in certain cases, where the terms of imprisonment were short; but now, I solemnly declare, that with no rewards or honours could I walk a happy man beneath the open sky by day, or lay me down upon my bed at night, with the consciousness that one human creature, for any length of time, no matter what, lay suffering this unknown punishment in his silent cell, and I the cause, or I consenting to it in the least degree.[1]

But Alexis de Tocqueville, on his earlier visit, in 1836, which he made together with Mr Crawford, one of the new inspectors of English prisons under the 1835 Act, approved of the system. Crawford's enthusiastic report led the Home Secretary, Lord John Russell, to initiate a Bill to establish a new national penitentiary organized on the Cherry Hill plan. The Bill became law in 1839 and it was preceded by a circular issued to all magistrates, which called attention to the particular advantages of the scheme. Russell's new penitentiary, Pentonville, carefully designed to facilitate treatment on Pennsylvanian lines, was completed in 1842. It is still in use as one of the major London prisons.

The Commissioners appointed by Russell to supervise the new prison clearly and definitely announced in their report of 1847 that 'the separation of one prisoner from another [was] the only sound basis upon which a reformatory discipline [could] be established with any reasonable hope of success'. Within six years of the completion of Pentonville, fifty-four prisons were erected on the same pattern, giving accommodation in separate cells for 11,000 prisoners. With very few exceptions, such as Wormwood Scrubs (1874), all the walled prisons now in use in Britain date from this period and are designed to the same basic plan. It is a simple plan: a series of corridors, on each side of which the cells are placed in tiers, radiate like the limbs of a star fish from a central point where the officers have an unrestricted view of any activities taking place on the landings.[2]

Pentonville was the second prison, after Millbank, to come directly under central control. The Home Secretary was now

[1] *American Notes.*
[2] See Appendix A for small provincial prison of this type.

responsible for convicts, i.e. those sentenced to transportation or
death, those in the hulks, and those in Millbank and in Pentonville. The second national penitentiary had been made necessary
by overcrowding at Millbank and in the hulks, but it was not
fully occupied by convicts. Some ordinary prisoners, serving
relatively short sentences, were confined there, but soon all
prisoners in Pentonville, without reference to the nature of their
crimes or to the duration of their imprisonment, were dealt with
according to the Pennsylvania system. Although the county
authorities equipped themselves with 'model prisons' on the
Pentonville pattern, not all as yet adopted the separate system in
its new form. The treadmill was still in use in some institutions,
whose controllers asked how hard labour, which they were bound
to apply, could be adapted to the cellular system.

There were some critics of the new Pentonville. Hepworth
Dixon, writing in 1850, says:

> It must be noted at the outset, that two accidents, for which,
> however, Mr Crawford cannot be blamed, go a long way to
> destroy our confidence in the correctness of his conclusions.
> In the first place, when he visited the United States nearly
> nineteen years ago, penal institutions, even there, were in
> their infancy. The Americans had not then accumulated such
> an amount of practical experience as is necessary to test the
> soundness of a moral theory so complicated as prison punish-
> ments by solitary confinement; and, of course, no nation in
> Europe had. In the second place, Mr Crawford had a strong,
> though perhaps an unconscious, leaning to the Philadelphian
> plan. The penitentiary had not . . . tried moral and religious
> instruction; how, then, could Mr Crawford tell, from its
> experience, that they would act well in union with the
> perfectly alien element of isolation? How could he infer from
> what he witnessed that the projected combination could be
> made 'powerfully instrumental, not only in deterring, but also
> in reclaiming the offender? Never was there a false deduc-
> tion.[1]

Hepworth Dixon gives an account of the design of Pentonville,
and the way in which it was run in his day, at the time when it
met with most general approval throughout the country:

[1] Hepworth Dixon, op. cit.

The building consists of five wings or galleries, radiating from a point, the view from which is very striking, and at the same time very unprisonlike. On the sides of four of these galleries the cells are situate and numbered. There are 520 of them, but not more than 500 are ever occupied. . . . Now let us enter a cell. Well, really, it has anything but a repulsive appearance. Its arrangement and fittings seem to be faultless. It is sufficiently large, being thirteen feet long, seven broad, and nine high. It is admirably ventilated, on the newest scientific principle, and by means of warm air is kept at an even and agreeable temperature. It has even the luxuries of a water-closet, and of an unlimited supply of warm and cold water.[1] The bedding is clean and good; the food is also good, and plentiful in supply. There is a bell-handle, too, which needs only to be pulled to command the instant attendance of a paid servitor. Light work is to be had also for amusement and to vary the routine. Very pleasant! At intervals the prisoner goes to chapel to hear the gospel; and to school, where competent masters are waiting to offer their services to instruct him. But what is there penal in all this? someone asks. For our life we cannot find out. . . .

The reader may be inclined to think that with so many expensive luxuries about him, the convict must consider Pentonville a very desirable place of sojourn. He does not, however. No prisoner, except in rare cases, likes it. Many fear it worse than they do death. . . . But then officials like it: it gives them very little trouble; so, without pretending to understand its complicated effects, moral or mental, they almost all swear by it. In fact, the model prison is the place exactly for the model warder. The men who have to bear its isolation think of it far differently. There are persons, well-meaning and honest, who pretend to think separation no great cruelty. Why do they not try it?

The prisoners sent to undergo the trial-discipline at Pentonville are selected—very carefully selected—from all the English gaols. The best in health, and in morals, and in good conduct are taken thither. They undergo a course of training for Pentonville, and are promoted to it. The surgeon of the

---

[1] Both long since removed from Pentonville, which in 1959 has 'recesses' as offensive as those in other English closed prisons.

F

gaol must first consider the candidate able to bear up against the weight of the separation; . . . then he must satisfy the chaplain, governor, and inspector of the prison to which he is confined, as to his moral and mental fitness to undergo and profit by the regimen. After all these preliminary examinations, he may be rejected by the officials at Pentonville itself.

While in prison, [convicts] are supposed not to see or know each other. This innocent delusion they themselves try to keep up. But the fact is – they know each other perfectly, and communicate both in voice and writing. Several cases of the sort have been detected. Last year, just one half of the prison punishments were inflicted for attempts to communicate. . . . In passing along the corridors, the men see each other's forms, motions, and as much of the face as they wish, in spite of the hood-beak, one of the paltriest expedients for self-deception ever invented. In the school room they hear each other's voices, one by one, and again and again, reading aloud. What greater facilities for mutual recognition could be given? The isolation of prisoners, even from each other, is all a dream.

Confining attention to the prison itself – it seems to work admirably. There is perfect order, perfect silence. The stillness of the grave reigns in every part. To a person accustomed to see only such gaols as Giltspur-street and Horsemonger-lane – with all their noise, filth, and disorder – the change is striking in the extreme. The observer feels as if he had come upon a new and different world. In the cell, he sees the prisoner calm, subdued, industriously at work upon his lessons or his labours. In the galleries and in the airing-grounds he also sees him quiet, downcast, obedient – very obedient. All this looks admirable. . . . The man who looks into it more narrowly will find the secrets of the good behaviour of the prisoner and of the order of the prison. The order comes from the silent ministration of the lock and key; the good conduct from the almost total absence of temptation of any kind to do wrong.

. . . In order to teach the untamed criminal to restrain the violence of his passions, [Pentonville] isolates him from his fellows, and proposes to give him the power of overcoming

temptation by removing him out of its reach! Of all questionable means to effect a given end, this seems to me the most
questionable. In the name of reason, what discipline can the
cell afford to the uneducated? . . . We have lunatics in strait-
jackets, very quiet and very harmless, who, if out of them,
would be very violent. But is this a good argument for
putting all lunatics, without exception, into strait-jackets?
The cell is, in fact, the criminal's strait-jacket. It keeps him
very quiet, makes him very obedient; but the question,
nevertheless, remains open – Does it make him a better man?
What we want are sound minds, not quiet men in strait-
jackets; good citizens, not submissive criminals in silent
cells. . . .

How far the discipline of Pentonville affects the mind, it
would be presumptuous to assert. Opinion is greatly divided
on that point. There can be no doubt, however, that it gives
a low, listless, melancholy expression to the face. Persons
who have placed themselves under its protection certainly
look subdued. Whether they all, after a time, pass into the
earlier stages of idiocy, as some assert, we know not. . . .
The first batch or two of men who were sent from Pentonville to the Australian colonies were literally unable to take
care of themselves on the voyage. A day or two after the
deadweight of silence and isolation was taken off, a great
number of them became half-idiotic . . .[1]

This was the institution to be emulated throughout Britain,
and this the form of treatment which thousands of men and
women convicted in the second half of the nineteenth century
were to undergo. Disease and ill health in prisons, accidentally
created by badly designed buildings badly sited, and allowed to
develop in the absence of firm rules and adequate supervision,
were now quickly to disappear from the prisons of England. In
their place we were to have huge, castellated structures so rigidly
ordered and disciplined that they ruined the minds of the men
pacing out life like a ritual within them.

[1] Mayhew, H. and Binny, J., *The Criminal Prisons of London* (London, 1862),
say, 'the discipline pursued at this prison [Pentonville] yields *upwards of ten
times more lunatics* than should be according to the normal rate'. (This state-
ment is based on statistics from December 1842 to December 1850.)

How can we, whose lives are blessed with continual
liberty, and upon whose will there is scarcely any restraint
– we, who can live among those we love, and move where we
list, we, to whom the wide world, with its infinite beauties
of sunshine, and beauty and form and air and colour and even
sound, are a perpetual fountain of health and joy; how can
we possibly comprehend what intense misery it is to be cut
off from all such enjoyments, to have our lives hemmed in by
four white blank walls – to see no faces but those of task
masters, to hear no voice but that of commanding officers,
to be denied all exercise of will whatever, and to be thwarted
into mere living automata forced to do the bidding of others?

asked a contemporary writer.

Without deliberation, in Pentonville the English had adopted
a new refinement of cruelty.

CHAPTER IX

CONVICT COLONIES

The arrival of Macquarie, in 1809, as Governor, began the first serious, planned attempt to develop the Australian penal settlements. Macquarie realized the enormous advantage to Australia of the large supply of skilled and unskilled labour pouring into it: an advantage which few other British colonies in new lands enjoyed in their early days. He had a big labour force entitled to little or no payment, with which he set about the construction of new towns beyond the reach of floods, and the building of good roads to connect the towns with one another and with the land beyond: 'The work was punitive, and was also beneficial to the whole public. No better employment could have been devised for the convicts.' Within a few months of his arrival, Macquarie, by the sheer force of his personality, had disciplined the rabble of convicts he found into a body of labourers who would obey orders and really work at the tasks they were given. Towns were established and linked together, and highways were built into wild, uninhabited and often unexplored regions, so that future settlers would find a sound scheme of communications ready for them if they could be persuaded to emigrate to the new continent. A vast road was erected across the Blue Mountains from the coast, spanning rivers and streams with high, solid, wooden bridges, for the entire length of its 276 miles. But in his isolation from the government at home, this dictatorial man pursued his schemes with single-minded enthusiasm, without advice from any other official, and ignorant of the experience which had been gained in earlier schemes of colonization elsewhere. And he was determined to leave as monuments behind him not only the sound, well-planned roads and harbours which were of practical use, but stately, impressive public buildings in the towns themselves, far larger, and absorbing far more of the limited wealth of the still poverty-stricken colony, than could possibly be justified at the time. Sydney, which he found as a mere shanty town, was

razed to the ground and redeveloped as a magnificent city, on a
street plan which it retains even to this day. Imposing houses
replaced the settlers' huts, and fine barracks the squalid dwellings
in which prisoners had formerly lived.

Macquarie's great error was to concentrate existing labour
forces in the towns, at a time when the economic need was for
extensive agricultural development over a wide area. He gave
a mean, underdeveloped little colony urban attractions which it
could not really afford until fifty or more years after his death,
and he may well have been an important contributor to one of
Australia's modern economic ills: the overweighting of the urban
population as compared with rural settlers in a nation which must
live mainly by its agriculture.

Settlers who arrived were unwilling to leave Macquarie's well-
laid-out towns for hard, unrewarding work in the hinterland,
despite the comparative ease of communication which road-
building works had ensured them.

The idea of making industrious agricultural workers out of
the freed convicts was ruined when they could barter away the
land awarded to them on discharge to a new settler in exchange
for rum. Large numbers of convicts were kept at work in the
towns themselves, building and extending them, and those already
released preferred to enjoy drunkenness and dissipation in the
dwellings thus created.

> Hence, though towns grew fast in beauty and importance,
> the forest lands or wild tracts in the interior remained un-
> settled . . . the condition of the towns was awful, and the low
> pleasures in which they abounded attracted to them many
> people who might otherwise have been content to live quietly
> upon their grants of land.

Macquarie was a good man, sincerely devoted to the work of
reforming the convicts in his charge; but he chose the wrong
means of doing so. He assumed that if he encouraged discharged convicts to take the land granted to them and to work on
it well, the opportunity would be accepted gladly, and that ex-
prisoners, given posts of some responsibility in his colony, would
become loyal and reliable. Within a year of his arrival he made
an ex-convict a Justice of the Peace and another his personal
doctor. The convicts were often the most clever and the most

well-educated men in the colony: neither the poor settlers who came on government grants, nor the officers who arrived with the prison ships, had been outstandingly successful at home. Macquarie's policies encouraged the worst ambitions among his former charges, not only the good.

Nevertheless, in the period of Macquarie's administration, from 1809 until 1821, the penal colony began to prosper. Although he encouraged free settlers far less than any of his predecessors, when he left Australia was a community more thriving, and more welcoming to men and women bent on a new life in a new country, than it had ever been.

His successor, Sir Thomas Brisbane, made great efforts to transform Australia from a predominantly penal colony into one in which the convicts might form merely a small section of the community. Under him, the first period of Australian history as a convict land came to an end. From the earliest days prisoners had been made available as labourers and servants to free men requiring assistance; Brisbane successfully attracted large numbers of settlers, to whom he assigned prisoners as workers.

Now had dawned the days of 'assignment' proper, the days of wholesale slavery, where private persons relieved the State of the charge of its criminals, and pretended to act, for the time being, as gaolers, taskmasters, and chaplains, in return for the labour supplied at so cheap a rate. How far the persons thus called upon to exercise such peculiar functions were entitled to the confidence reposed in them was never in question until the last days.

Settlers who required free labour made formal application to an Assignments Board set up under the Governor's authority, which had absolute power to award male and female convicts to private citizens. As each ship docked, prisoners were marched to the convict barracks in Sydney, to parade before the Governor and await allocation by the Assignments Board to their new masters.

The employers had no choice of the men or women given them: they asked for a certain number, of a specified sex, gambling on the health and ability of the prisoners they might receive. And the responsibility of transporting the 'servants' to their farms, workshops or homes lay upon the employer. Under the Transportation Act, the Governor of the colony had complete control over the prisoners: on assigning them, he made them over as property, to be moved about, fed, clothed, made to work and punished just as the settler concerned might wish.

Some masters treated their convict slaves well, either from genuine humanity or as a bribe for good work, and a few prisoners may well have been better looked after than they had been by their employers in freedom at home. But all were called upon to be instantly submissive to the men who owned their labour, or to the ex-convicts sometimes employed as overseers. Until 1835 no inquiry as to the character of settlers applying for assigned labour was made. They might be sadistic or merely harsh, or on the other hand completely unable to exercise control.

Those prisoners who had not been assigned for labour remained at the convict barracks in Sydney, or, in the case of women, at the so-called Paramatta Factory. At both establishments, little work was organized, and little check was kept on the behaviour and movements of the inmates. The convicts were not even locked up at night.

The officers at the barracks were tampered with, and winked for substantial reasons at the nightly evasions of the prisoners in their charge . . . gross peculation and embezzlement were continually practised [and] . . . in this universal slackness of control, the lower officials battened and grew rich at the public expense.[1]

As a result of the policy of assignment, and despite the opportunities for profiteering at public expense, which developed during his period of office, Sir Thomas Brisbane was able to claim that the cost to Britain of maintaining the convict colony was substantially reduced. He offered grants of land up to two thousand acres to any new settler willing to employ twenty convicts. Supplies of food for the settlers' families and their prisoners were given from government stores for the first six months after arrival, and cattle were lent from the government's own herds. In these circumstances, with free land, free labour and free food until they could become established, the immigrant population rose sharply. Shortly after Brisbane's successor, Sir Ralph Darling, arrived, the demand for slaves had increased to a point where it exceeded supply, and the barracks in Sydney were besieged by

[1] Griffiths, op. cit.

claimants as each new transport ship arrived. Darling attempted to bring some order to the confused system of assignment which Brisbane left, and was responsible for one clear reform: an insistence that land would only be granted in future to people who were well able to farm efficiently and who could therefore provide adequate work for the convicts they employed.

Sir Richard Bourke, the last Governor of New South Wales as a penal colony, arrived in 1831, to institute, in the last days of assignment, the most satisfactory system of administering such an undesirable institution which could have been devised. Four years after his arrival, and only five before assignment was to be abandoned, he introduced a measure to 'substitute for the invidious distinction hitherto more or less vested in the officers entrusted with the duty of assigning convicts to private service, strict rules of qualification intelligible alike to the dispenser and receiver of penal labour, and from which no deviation shall be permitted . . .'[1]

The basic principle of the new regulations was that the number of servants allocated to each applicant would be determined by the area of land he held, at a rate of one prisoner to 160 acres of uncultivated land, and one to 20 acres under cultivation. Since mechanics were more valuable in the colony than ordinary labourers, every skilled man would equal two labourers (or three, depending on his trade and ability). A completely new method of application for labour was also introduced. Requests were to be made to district magistrates sitting in special session each September, who would

> inquire into the correctness of the facts stated in each, requiring such evidence thereof, as to them shall seem proper; and they shall in no case recommend the claim of any applicant unless perfectly satisfied of the truth of the statement on which the application is founded.

No person 'who is not free, of good character, capable of maintaining the servants applied for, and to whose care and management they may not be safely entrusted' might be awarded prisoners. The actual assignments were made by drawing lots from a box in the Assignment Board offices under the new system, so that it was impossible for the officials to show favour.

[1] *Despatch*, June 1835.

Bourke was the most clear-sighted and efficient of the administrators into whose care the Australian colonies had up to this time been placed. Indeed, several years before it occurred, he foresaw the realization of Brisbane's dream as a practical possibility: an entirely free New South Wales, without convict labour.

CHAPTER X

THE END OF
TRANSPORTATION

Transportation had been resumed, after the discovery of Australia, in spite of strong opposition from men and women outside the government who were deeply concerned with the mental and physical improvement of prisoners. It had been welcomed by a government anxious for relief from the burden of instituting new, untried methods of treating convicted criminals at a time when the number of offences committed each year was steadily growing. In the Australian colonies, convicts were out of the minds of most people at home, as well as out of sight. During the early years of transportation to the antipodes, literate and observant witnesses of the scheme in practice, other than officials connected with its administration, hardly existed. In the American colonies there had been a large population of civilian settlers whose written comments and occasional visits to England kept some of the public at home aware of conditions in the penal settlements there. Australia was farther away, and until the end of Brisbane's governorship it had insufficient free settlers of education and social conscience to allow the growth of any feeling of communal responsibility for the horrific treatment of the convicts in their midst.

In the 1830's there was an awakening in New South Wales. Bourke's rationalization of the assignment system found support with many of the colonists from good families and of modest wealth who were being attracted there, many of whom refused to employ the slave labour at first so freely offered. The behaviour of emancipated convicts and of the predatory colonists who took extreme advantage of prisoners given into their care, stirred up fierce antagonism between them and the better type of settler now arriving. Some emancipated prisoners had already risen to power and influence. In some parts of the colony they ran most of the shops and other businesses. They had control of several newspapers, owned public-houses, and even did jury service. Inevitably, this was resented by the comparatively poor new arrivals who came to Australia honestly and of their own free will.

Crime was prevalent throughout the colony, much of it committed or encouraged by freed convicts; the number of convictions for highway robbery each year equalled the total of *all* convictions for *all* offences in England. The Police Magistrate of Sydney, in his report for 1835, pointed out that of the whole population in that city (some twenty thousand) the majority were prisoners, past or present,

> whose passions are violent, and who have not been accustomed to control them, yet for the most part have no lawful means of gratifying them. It includes a great number of incorrigible bad characters, who on obtaining their freedom will not apply themselves to any honest mode of earning their living, but endeavour to support themselves in idleness and debauchery by plunder. . . . There is no town which affords so much facility for eluding the vigilance of the police. The unoccupied bush near and within the town itself will afford shelter to the offender and hide him from pursuit; he may steal or hire a boat, and in a few minutes place an arm of the sea between him and his pursuers. . . . The drunkenness, idleness, and carelessness of a great portion of the inhabitants afford innumerable opportunities and temptations by day and night to live by plunder. . . .

This report was endorsed by the Chief Justice of the colony, who said in his own report that the accuracy of the Police Magistrate's remarks as a true description of the actual state of Sydney could not be denied.

Another Judge, Burton, raised his voice that year against transportation. He attributed the alarming extent of crime in New South Wales to masters of convict labour who were unable to control their enforced servants or who deliberately encouraged them to go out in armed bands of five or six to rob. Burton claimed that the cessation of transportation, together with increased inducements for ordinary, honest people to settle in New South Wales, was the only solution. The Australian colonies could never rise to their full status and achieve the free institutions for which many of their peoples had been clamouring, unless transportation was ended.

One of the visitors from England, who returned to comment bitterly on Australian penal conditions (in 1836), was a member of Elizabeth Fry's original Newgate Committee. With permission from the Governor to travel freely and to investigate the convicts' conditions where she would, this anonymous lady became increasingly horrified by the extent to which the treatment of transported convicts depended on the chance of their assignment to a good or bad master. She was also impressed by the protests against transportation made by many of the new colonists to whom she spoke. On her return to England, she reverted to John Howard's technique by publishing a book at her own expense, hoping thereby to arouse public opinion.[1] Her work, combined with the official reports of unrest in New South Wales arriving at the Colonial Office, inspired the appointment of a Select Committee of the House of Commons (under Sir William Molesworth) in 1837 to investigate the system anew. After the report of this committee the following year, transportation as a penal instrument entered its last and final stage.

The government's difficulty was to devise an alternative to transportation. The only convict prison in Britain was Millbank, and it was clearly impossible to divert the whole stream of transportees into the Thames hulks, which were already overcrowded and the subject of considerable political agitation. The compromise policy finally adopted, was to abandon transportation to New South Wales entirely, but to use Van Diemen's Land (Tasmania), which had already been receiving some convicts, as the main penal settlement. Moreover, the practice of assignment was to cease, and a system of 'probation' was to be applied to all transported prisoners.

Van Diemen's Land was now to become little more than a prison island: the whole colony was to be 'permeated, inundated, swamped with the criminal classes'. In the four years from the 20th of May 1840, when the new system came into operation, sixteen thousand convicts were sent there. The average number of prisoners in the island each year was thirty thousand, nearly twice the population of free, voluntary settlers.

[1] *The Prisoners of Australia*, by Miss A— (London, 1837).

The probation system introduced five stages, of increasing leniency, through which convicts were to pass. These were:

1. Detention in secure imprisonment at a purely penal institution on the island;
2. Removal to gangs engaged in government construction work in different parts of the island under maximum restraint;
3. Restricted freedom on a pass to seek work for themselves;
4. The award of a ticket of leave, allowing the convict to come and go as he pleased;
5. Absolute pardon.

The first stage was restricted to the worst criminals only; these were held at Norfolk Island and at Tasman's Peninsula. It was to last not less than two, and not more than four years, but flagrant misconduct would condemn an offender to an indefinite term of sentence, at the Governor's discretion. It was under this arrangement that transportation produced its most outstanding administrator and its most important contribution to penal ideas. Alexander Maconochie, who became superintendent of Norfolk Island in 1840, astonished his superiors by running it as a shamelessly reformative institution. He introduced a 'Marks System', under which it was possible for a prisoner, by his own efforts, to shorten the time he spent in the first stage. Marks were awarded according to the willingness with which an inmate worked, and the placidity of his behaviour; and the more speedily he was awarded marks, the more quickly came the day of his release. This idea was applied to men who had been sentenced at home to life imprisonment for the most heinous offences: by abandoning painful punishments altogether, and appealing in a remarkably effective way to the better feelings of the prisoners, Maconochie showed that the conception of progressive stages of detention could become a powerful inducement to good behaviour.

Within three years of its establishment the Van Diemen's Land scheme was clearly ineffective: Maconochie's good work, unrecognized at the time and, in fact, severely criticized for its leniency a few years later, affected only one of the two comparatively small first-stage institutions. The result of flooding the island with convict labour was a mass exodus of free colonists and the virtual bankruptcy of the colonial government. It was useless to attempt to prepare prisoners for free work when there was no work available for them to do, and when the farms and businesses previously built up by colonists were being abandoned. Even a large and already prosperous colony could hardly have found sufficient work for the thousands of prisoners who poured in each year. To make matters worse, the government in Britain insisted that all settlers hiring prison labour (including the public works department of the colony) should pay a tax over and above the normal wages of each convict engaged. This, at a time when the depressed employers could hardly afford ordinary wages.

The welfare of the probation system was certainly not ignored at home. Gladstone, when he became Under Secretary of State at the Colonial Office, advocated a scheme to relieve overcrowding in Van Diemen's Land by starting yet another penal colony in Northern Australia, but his government went out of office before it could be established. Grey, the new Colonial Secretary, revoked the plan, as 'impolitic and unnecessary', and attempted to mitigate the immediate confusion in Van Diemen's Land by suspending transportation altogether for two years (1846). It was now arranged that all men sentenced to transportation should undergo a set period of separate confinement in an institution such as the new Pentonville, at home; that they should then be allocated to labour in association on public works in Britain, Gibraltar or Bermuda, from which they might eventually be sent on ticket-of-leave to any colony which might be prepared to receive them. This plan was the origin of the sentence of Penal Servitude which came to dominate British penal treatment at the end of the nineteenth century. It was the need for more accommodation at home in the first stage which stimulated the building of Portland Prison (opened in 1850), and the conversion of Dartmoor, by rebuilding some of the halls as cellular structures, into a convict prison.

The first batch of men to be transported under the new arrangements left England in 1849, but the scheme had a very brief life. In 1852 Van Diemen's Land refused to accept criminals from the mother country, and Bermuda and Gibraltar, where there were already about 8,000 convicts, could not be used as receptacles for the numbers which might have been diverted to them instead. In 1853 *The Penal Servitude Act* substituted sentences of four years' penal servitude for the existing ones of seven years' transportation.

The adamant refusal of colonists in Van Diemen's Land to accept more convicts had been followed by urgent searches for other remote parts of the world to which they might be sent. An approach to Queensland was instantly repudiated, and brought forth an inquiry as to whether criminals from that colony might be sent to the British Isles instead. The Falkland Islands, Labrador and New Guinea were all suggested, unsuccessfully. The consequent discharge of many ticket-of-leave holders in Britain itself, led to impressive public agitation for an alternative scheme. Following upon a Select Committee of the House of Commons, the second *Penal Servitude Act* (1857) recommended that the terms of Penal Servitude should correspond exactly to previous sentences of transportation, and that there should be some remission in the case of convicts whose behaviour in prison was satisfactory. The portion of a sentence subject to remission depended upon the time to be served: one-sixth in the case of the minimum sentence of three years, and one-third in the case of a fifteen-year or longer sentence. This, the most severe type of prison sentence awarded in Great Britain, remained with us until the Criminal Justice Act of 1948.

Penal Servitude made it necessary for the government to take control, centrally, of no less than five prisons: Pentonville, Millbank, Parkhurst, Portland and Dartmoor. It was the first step to the inevitable conclusion, reached in 1877, of putting the entire penal system for adults under national administration.

CHAPTER XI

THE LONDON PRISONS

The prisons of London in 1855 were more numerous and more varied in function than at any time before. Pentonville, still awesomely regarded as a model, was directly under government control as a convict prison devoted mainly to men serving the first stage of their sentences under the Act of 1853. Millbank, also administered from the Home Office, took other convicts, who were submitted there to a 'mixed system' of discipline, which combined separate cellular confinement by night with silent work in association by day.

In 1849, four years after Elizabeth Fry's death, the foundation-stone of the new prison at Holloway had been laid and inscribed with an aim which paid no lip service to the ideas of Mrs Fry and her friends:

> May God preserve the City of London, and make this place *a terror* to evil doers.

Wandsworth Prison was opened as the Surrey House of Correction, in 1851. It had 'nothing to commend it to the eye,' writes a contemporary, 'none of the fine gloomy solemnity of Newgate, nor any of the castellated grandeur of the City Prison at Holloway . . .' It took offenders serving comparatively short sentences, both men and women. It had no treadmill, not because of any special humanity on the part of the magistrates responsible, but because they considered that such a device would prove too expensive to operate under the separate system. Prisoners sentenced to hard labour were put to work in the pump-house, where twelve stalls stood on each side of the building, each with a handle connected to the main pump. Nearly five thousand revolutions of the handles were required of each prisoner per day, to push water up into the cisterns on the roof. Some men, less fortunate, worked out the days in their cells, revolving the crank handles of hard-labour machines which produced nothing but exhaustion of body and boredom of mind.[1] Other prisoners at Wandsworth, sentenced to simple imprisonment, spent their time in tailoring, shoemaking, matmaking and picking coir. Women were occupied with needlework, cleaning and laundering.

Brixton, another Surrey House of Correction (which Wandsworth had been expected to supersede), was built in 1820 for female prisoners sentenced to hard labour. Hepworth Dixon, writing in 1850, said of it:

> Though, for London, it is not a large prison, it is in some respects rather a notable one. It is the only gaol in the capital into which the innovating and reforming spirit of the last ten or twelve years has failed to penetrate: it is entirely a treadwheel prison;[2] it enjoys the reputation of being very disorderly; it is unhealthy in spite of its admirable situation; and it is almost inaccessible to public inspection and control.

In 1853, following the Act of that year, Brixton prison was given over for use as a convict prison. Under this régime, the women wore 'a loose dark and claret-brown robe or gown with a blue check apron and neckerchief, and were surmounted with a cap of small close white muslin'. As far as possible the strict regulations of Pentonville were applied, but separation was not carried into the chapel, where the prisoners sat on ordinary seats, not in individual boxes. In 1854, punishments at Brixton, which was designed to hold 175 women (although after 1853 some occasionally had to sleep three in a cell), exceeded 1,200. Thirty-two women were kept in handcuffs and strait-jacket, and 288 confined in the almost totally dark punishment cells for days or weeks at a time.

Holloway Prison was completed in 1852. Like Wandsworth, it

---

[1] The crank, invented at Pentonville in 1846 especially for use in cellular prisons, was intended to supplant the treadmill but was often used together with it. The machine is described as 'a narrow iron drum placed on legs, with a long handle on one side which, when turned, causes a series of cups or scoops in the interior to revolve. At the lower part of the interior of the machine is a thick layer of sand, which the cups, as they come round, scoop up, and carry to the top of the wheel, where they throw it out and empty themselves, after the principle of a dredging machine. A dial-plate, fixed in front of the iron drum, shows how many revolutions the machine has made. It is usual to shut up in a cell the man sent to crank labour, so that the exercise is rendered doubly disagreeable by the solitude.' Mayhew, H. and Binny, J., *The Criminal Prisons of London* (London, 1862).

[2] The treadwheel had been installed at a cost of £7,000.

was designed on the Pentonville pattern, with separate cells in radial wings, but it was controlled and administered by the Common Council of the City of London. As a correctional institution, it took both men and women serving short sentences. It had accommodation for 350 inmates in seven wings, each of which was intended to hold prisoners of a different type. When the building of Holloway was begun in 1849, it was intended to replace Newgate, the old gaol in which Elizabeth Fry had started her reforming work, but so great was the pressure upon prison accommodation in London, that Newgate remained until the end of the century.

Newgate, still with its large old wards, and almost unchanged in physical structure since 1813, remained after the opening of Holloway primarily as a place of detention for men and women awaiting trial at the Central Criminal Court. In 1857, while it was still in use, reconstruction began: by 1861 Elizabeth Fry's demand of fifty years earlier, for separate cells in Newgate, had been met. It continued as a place of detention for prisoners as yet untried and awaiting execution, until 1901, when condemned men were sent to Brixton Prison instead, and the old prison was demolished in order to build the present 'Old Bailey' on its site.

Clerkenwell Prison (officially the House of Detention for the County of Middlesex) performed much the same functions as Brixton Prison today. The foundation-stone of the new building was laid in 1849, and it was designed almost exactly as a replica of Pentonville. There had been a prison on the site since 1775, when a model prison roughly approaching the early ideas of John Howard on prison design was erected. Howard described this with some approbation in *The State of the Prisons*. In 1818, the building was demolished, to be replaced with a larger one. Thus, the radial prison of 1849 was the third on the same site, at the end of Farringdon Street. Its function was purely as a place of detention for prisoners awaiting the Assizes, who wore their own clothes and were not required to do any work other than the general cleaning and other tasks necessary to keep the building in good order.

Horsemonger Lane, the prison to which Leigh Hunt was committed for describing George IV as 'an Adonis of fifty', was built in Lambeth at the instigation of John Howard. It was the main county prison for Surrey. There were ten separate communal wards for inmates of different character, each with its own segregated exercise yard. But Hepworth Dixon reported:

> The visitor is painfully impressed with the absence of all rule and system in the management . . . Here there is no attempt to enforce discipline. Neither silence nor separation is maintained in the largest prison in the metropolitan county of Surrey! . . . some prisoners clearly prefer their present state of idleness: with hands in their pockets, they saunter about their dungeon, or loll upon the floor, listening to the highly spiced stories of their companions, well content to be fed at the expense of the county – upon a better diet, better cooked, than they are accustomed to at home – without any trouble or exertion on their own part. . . . We have no hesitation in saying, that, to the worst sort of offenders, Horsemonger Lane gaol presents attractions rather than terrors.

Picking oakum was the only work available on the men's side of the prison, but there was hardly sufficient even of this degrading work for them to do. 'By twelve or one o'clock many have finished, and the rest of the day is given up to laziness.'

Coldbath Fields was a Middlesex County House of Correction in the district between Clerkenwell and Pentonville. It was originally built in the reign of James I, but in 1794 a second building on the same site was erected, and this, with considerable additions, was the prison which stood in 1855. From its earliest days, Coldbath Fields had a reputation for unusual severity of treatment. Coleridge referred to it as a place worse than hell:

> *As he went through Coldbath Fields, he saw*
> *A solitary cell;*
> *And the devil was pleased, for it gave him a hint*
> *For improving his prisons in hell.*

In 1854 the prison contained 1,495 inmates, less than a thousand of whom were held in separate cells. The remainder were in rooms shared by four or five prisoners together. The governorship of this enormous institution was 'usually conferred upon persons who have served with success in the army or navy – strict disciplinarians, men who have learned to obey as well as been used

Tothill Fields Prison, *c.* 1850, showing shielded cell windows

to command . . . The official staff consisted of the governor, two chaplains, one medical officer, three trade instructors, and 134 assistant officers', a body of men considered 'rather too small than too large considering the nature of the duties devolving upon it'.[1]

The prison was managed on the silent associated system, with the treadmill and oakum or coir picking as the main punishment. The treadmill at Coldbath Fields revolved at the rate of thirty-two feet per minute, and the prisoners worked on it for six hours a day, for periods of three hours. Oakum picking was done in an enormous room accommodating 500 inmates, and in complete silence. '. . . if a man rested for a moment, he was encouraged and cheered to further industry by seeing on the walls the improving texts, "It is good for a man that he bear the yoke in his youth"; "Godliness with contentment is a great gain"; "Go to the ant, thou sluggard, consider her ways to be wise".' In 1854, of a total population of 9,180, over 9,000 prisoners were punished at Coldbath Fields, most of them for minor deviations from the rules, such as 'noise making' and 'bad language'. Nevertheless, considering 'the disorderly habits of the mass of persons sent to this prison, and the shortness of the terms for which they are committed – the cleanliness, order and industry prevailing in it are highly creditable to its governor and officers. In many important respects, it is the best of our metropolitan gaols.'[2]

Tothill Fields Prison was originally a bridewell, erected in 1618. When John Howard visited it he found a motto carved over the doorway:

HERE are several sorts of work for the poor of this parish of ST MARGARET'S, WESTMINSTER, and also the county according to law, and for such as will beg and live idly in this city of WESTMINSTER.

He described it as a remarkably well-managed institution, and, indeed, it was in a very pleasant situation. 'It appears to be embosomed in a very enviable grove of trees; to the casual glance, suggesting shadier nooks and softer siestas than are always to be found among the cushions and benches of Bellamy's and the Houses [of Parliament].' The prison was rebuilt in 1835, on the

[1] In Wormwood Scrubs Prison, in 1959, with approximately the same number of inmates, the staff of uniformed officers is no larger.
[2] Hepworth Dixon, op. cit. (1850).

same site, south of Victoria Street and near Vauxhall Bridge Road. From 1850 onward it was restricted to convicted female prisoners and boys under the age of seventeen, all other male prisoners from the Westminster district being sent to Coldbath Fields. There was room for 300 boys and nearly 600 women, only about half of whom had a solitary cell for sleeping. But despite the pleasant impression it gave from the outside, and Howard's favourable comments a century before, Tothill Fields was extremely unhealthy. In 1854 nearly half the prisoners were perpetually sick and unfit for work.

A contemporary writer who protested against 'the strong and injurious disposition to convert our gaols into institutions for inducing mere moral reformation, rather than penance' was able to praise the juvenile section of this institution highly. With some appreciation he noted that 11 per cent. of the boys were placed in dark punishment cells during the year, and that they were in general more roughly treated than the adults by the gaolers.[1]

The chief work provided for the boys and the women was oakum picking,

a very unequal punishment. To the young offender it is a severe punishment, breaking his nails and tearing the flesh off his finger-ends. . . . The old criminals, having been often in gaol, have acquired, by long practice, a knack of getting the oakum through their fingers very quickly. For the hardened criminal it has no terrors.

Tothill Fields, Clerkenwell, Coldbath Fields, Horsemonger Lane and Millbank[2] are now abolished. The buildings of Pentonville, Wandsworth, Brixton and Holloway remain in use to this day, substantially unaltered in design. Only one London prison, Wormwood Scrubs, which was begun in 1874 with convict labour from Millbank, has been added since. Not one has been erected in London (indeed, only four have been built anywhere in the country) since full responsibility for all prisons was placed directly under the Home Office in 1877.

[1] There were usually some 2,500 youths under seventeen years of age committed to this particular prison, and of these more than 200 had been convicted at least four times previously. The theft of goods costing merely a few pence could bring a sentence of imprisonment upon a child in the mid-nineteenth century.

[2] Millbank Prison was closed on 6 November 1890, and pulled down in 1903. The Tate Gallery now stands on part of the site.

CHAPTER XII

THE BIRMINGHAM SCANDAL

Although the separate system instituted at Pentonville in 1842 met with the full approval of the Inspectors of Prisons, who encouraged its introduction throughout the country, and all prisons built after that time were of a cellular kind, the argument for and against separation continued in the Press, among prominent reformers and in the House of Commons. It was not until the Prison Act of 1865 was passed that cellular confinement became absolutely and firmly entrenched into the English prison system, to remain unquestioned for the remainder of the century. Pentonville Prison and the treatment it practised under the Penal Servitude Act of 1857 became the models to which the majority of prisons in Britain, still under county and city control, gradually, with the advice and encouragement of the inspectors and the encroachment of Home Office regulations, approximated. The condition of the various prisons in London in 1855 has indicated how widely different the lives of prisoners could be at that time even in one city. Just as in modern times some counties have an unusually good reputation for the educational services they provide, while others lag a little behind the average standard, in mid-Victorian times the efficiency of prison administration, with the state institution of Pentonville as a yardstick, depended upon the interest and enthusiasm of local authorities, and upon the money they were able or willing to expend upon it.

Five years after the opening of Pentonville, the relative values of the separate and silent systems were still under discussion at the Brougham Committee of the House of Lords, whose task was to consider criminal justice with special reference to juvenile offenders. The chaplain of Preston Prison proclaimed cellular isolation to be 'the only possible basis for a system of reformation'. Captain Maconochie, now in England again, strongly opposed it. He declared that the inmates of Pentonville were in a

87

state of complete mental and physical exhaustion, and incapable
of reformation under the régime. Nevertheless, in 1857 the Inspectors of Prisons announced in their report that

> so universal . . . is the testimony in favour of the Separate
> System in English prisons [in the south and west] that there
> remain only two county prisons [there] in which it has not
> been adopted, either wholly or in part; and in those ex-
> ceptional instances new buildings are now in progress,
> which promise soon to assimilate them to the more perfect
> establishments of the kind.

As we have seen, of the institutions under local control in London,
only the City of London House of Correction at Holloway maintained complete separation. The authorities of Surrey and Middlesex were thought very backward.

But this final twenty years under the local authorities saw some
fertile experiments. In particular, Maconochie, the man who had
made such a unique contribution toward penal administration in
the last stage of transportation to Van Diemen's Land, stood out
as an official who, by unorthodox methods in one local prison,
influenced the development of national policy. In his brief period
as governor of Birmingham Prison, from 1849 until 1851, he put
into operation the Marks System he had developed at Norfolk
Island. The scheme was explained in his book, *Crime and Punishment*, published in 1846:

> In the management of our gaols and other places of punish-
> ment, we at present attach too much importance to mere
> submission and obedience. We make the discipline in them
> military, overlooking a distinction . . . to which too much
> importance cannot be attached, between the objects of mili-
> tary and improved penal discipline. The ultimate purpose of
> military discipline, is to train men to act together; but that of
> penal discipline is to prepare them advantageously to separate.
> The objects being thus opposite, the processes should equally
> differ: but we make them the same, and reap accordingly.
> A good prisoner, it has been observed, is usually a bad man,
> and in the circumstances this result is sufficiently intelligible.
> Men kept for weeks, months, years, under a severe external
> pressure, and praised and encouraged in proportion as they

submit to it, are in a direct course of preparation to yield to
other forms of pressure as soon as they present themselves.
They go in weak, or they would not probably be prisoners,
and they come out still more enfeebled.

The whole organization of the Marks System, then, is
directed to cure this defect in our present penal arrangements.
It offers wages (marks) to stimulate to voluntary as opposed
to compulsory exertion; it imposes fines in the same currency
to deter from, rather than otherwise prevent misconduct;
it charges in them for supplies issued, in order to create an
interest in voluntary moderation, and it promises the recovery
of liberty only to a definite accumulation of them, over and
above all that may be thus expended, thereby affording the
strongest stimulus to systematic exertion, prudence and self-
command the virtues best suited to sustain men against
external temptation after discharge. The qualities of immediate
obedience and submission are thus not sacrificed, for the
absence of them may entail corresponding fines: but they are
obtained by the exercise of the higher virtues, not by their
being placed in abeyance – and will cultivate what they thus
exhibit.

Maconochie had the opportunity to describe his system in a
more detailed manner when he was called to appear before Lord
Grey's Committee on Prison Discipline in 1850. The Marks System
had not been welcomed by those most concerned with prison
administration; indeed, the version of it which he applied at Norfolk Island had won him no credit among his superiors. The
apparent leniency with which he was able to treat criminals under
his control created for him many envious enemies. The short trial
Maconochie was able to give his theories at Birmingham Prison
ended abruptly when he was called upon to support his deputy
in a policy of greater severity.

To the Committee of 1850, Maconochie explained his belief:

Time sentences are at the root of very nearly all the demorali-
zation which exists in prisons. A man under a time sentence
thinks only how he is to cheat that time, and while it away;
he evades labour, because he has no interest in it whatever,
and he has no desire to please the officers under whom he is
placed, because they cannot serve him essentially; they cannot

in any way promote his liberation. Besides this, in the desire
to while away his time, he conjures up in his mind, and in-
dulges, when he has the opportunity, in every sort of prurient
and stimulative thought, and word, and even, where he can,
act . . . Now the whole of these evils would be remedied by
introducing the system of task sentences. A man under a task
sentence would . . . set a proper value upon time, which
under a time sentence is hated, and he would exert himself in
such a way that he could not but improve, *he must improve.*
The difficulty in imposing task sentences is the finding a
general expression for labour. *I have proposed marks to represent
labour* . . . If the Secretary of State were to say that ten marks
a day, as a matter of course, should be the expression for
good fair average labour in a gaol, and were to give directions
to governors and Visiting Justices to accommodate their
calculations of piece work to that scale, I experience myself
no difficulty whatever in so gaining a universal expression,
and I think that no difficulty whatsoever to earn it . . . There
would be a constant stimulus to effort, on the one hand, to
gain marks, and to self-denial on the other, to retain them. . . .

Sentences would take the form of imposing upon the offender a
'debt' of 3,000 marks, for example, and 'until he could earn them
he would show himself unfit to return to society, by wanting that
diligence and industry, and exertion and prudence, which are the
only means by which a poor man can keep out of gaol'.[1]

In appointing Maconochie as governor of the new gaol at
Birmingham, the Justices responsible particularly desired him to
give his system the proof of trial. But soon afterwards they
objected to the unaccustomed lack of military discipline it en-
tailed, and took away from him the responsibility for much of the
routine administration of the institution. His deputy governor,
Lieutenant Austin, into whose hands it was placed, instituted over
the head of his own governor a régime of the utmost severity.
Protests from Maconochie in 1851 brought the offer of Austin's
resignation, which the Justices refused to accept, demanding instead that the governor himself should go. In this way, the
Justices of Birmingham made themselves the subject of one of the
most shameful scandals in British prison history.

[1] Webb, S. and B., op. cit.

A little over a year after Maconochie had left Birmingham, rumours of brutality in the prison circulated. Unusual punishments were mentioned by the prison chaplain at the inquest on a prisoner who had hanged himself,[1] and these remarks attracted the attention of one of the government inspectors. Following upon an unsatisfactory report by the local magistrates on the subject, a Royal Commission was set up to investigate the whole administration of the establishment. The report of the Commission, published in 1854, proved that Austin had practised deliberate cruelty upon the prisoners in his charge. Labour in the prison was performed on a special type of crank, invented in Leicester Prison, which caused far greater strain to the prisoners than was apparent to a casual inspector. Ten thousand daily revolutions on this machine were required. If an inmate was unable to complete this task, he was made to stay in the crank cell all night without food. A special type of strait-jacket was employed to deal with hysterical violence among prisoners who were unable to meet this tortuous routine: a jacket which was described by the not-over-sympathetic members of the Commission as 'an engine of positive torture'.

The Commission decided that the suicide at Birmingham was in fact 'a deliberate act of self-destruction, committed by the prisoner to relieve himself from bodily and mental suffering'. 'We are of the opinion', they said, 'that by the order and with the knowledge of the governor [Austin], he was punished illegally and cruelly, and was driven thereby to the commission of suicide.' Other examples of brutality carried out by Maconochie's successor included the whipping of two disobedient boys, carried out continually, day by day, *'and so on, until the boy became obedient'*. The Commissioners formally recorded their disapproval of such inflictions. 'The notion of persevering in the infliction of bodily pain day after day until by its repetition the "obstinacy" of a prisoner is subdued, appears to be opposed to every principle upon which punishment ought to be administered.'

The report went on to criticize the medical officer:

... his examination of prisoners on their admission, one object of which ought certainly to have been the ascertaining whether they were in a fit state to undergo the ordinary

[1] The novel, *It's Never too Late to Mend,* by Charles Reade (London, 1856), is based on this and other contemporary incidents at Birmingham Prison.

discipline, and to perform the ordinary labour, seems to have been made in a most careless and superficial manner, and without any reference to that question . . . his inspections of prisoners, when performed, were of such a character as to be generally quite useless as means of detecting illness, [so] that although instances of great suffering and injury to health from excessive labour and want of food must constantly have come under his notice, he rarely interfered to relieve the prisoners from the operations of a discipline and modes of punishment which few could have been capable of supporting ! . .

Of Captain Maconochie, the Commissioners said:

. . . we are fully satisfied that he is a gentleman of humanity and benevolence, whose sole object in undertaking the government of the prison, was to promote the reformation of the prisoners, and the well-being of society, by means of the system of moral discipline which he hoped to establish there.

But of Lieutenant Austin:

. . . he appears almost from the first to have adopted the notion, that the principle of strict separation, combined with hard labour, was to be effectually maintained by no other means than by the instant infliction of punishment for every infraction of the discipline or failure in the labour; and we have already seen that, not content with the administration of punishments authorized by the law . . . he introduced of his own authority another, not only illegal, but most objectionable from its painful, cruel, and exasperating character, which he practised with a frequency distressing to hear of, for offences too trivial to call for any severity of punishment at all, and upon offenders quite unfit to be subjected to it, combining with it also other inflictions and privations, and directing and witnessing their application with a lamentable indifference to human suffering, until the penal system of the gaol became almost a uniform system of the application of pain and terror . . .

The revelations of the Royal Commission upon the activities of Austin (who, together with Blount, was brought to trial) aroused a storm of indignation in the Press. The crass carelessness and in-

Treadmill and oakum-picking shed at Holloway Prison, 1862

efficiency it revealed in the Visiting Magistrates led the people of
Birmingham to demand the appointment of a Stipendiary in their
place. But Birmingham was only one prison to which the horrified
attention of the public had been almost accidentally drawn.

> It should for ever make for humility in prison administrators
> [said the Webbs] to reflect that it is doubtful whether the sum
> of human suffering was not in this period, during long
> stretches of years, greater at Millbank and Pentonville peni-
> tentiaries, than at the worst of the prisons under Local
> Government.[1]

We had what John Howard and Elizabeth Fry had longed for:
some prisons, at least, which were efficiently run according to a
deliberate policy, and inspected by government officials to ensure
that that policy was carried out. The tragedy is that in the most
efficient and most thoroughly inspected of them, the wrong
policy, a slow grinding down of the minds of men, was being
pursued.

The public interest which the Birmingham scandal had aroused
was of enormous value to the cause of prison reform. It focused
attention on prisoners, and the way they were, and should be,
treated, and it strengthened in many minds the view that *all* penitentiaries, in whatever part of the country they were situated, and
whatever type of offender they received, should be placed under
central control. Moreover, it placed Maconochie in a favourable
light as compared with his successor, and made his views circulate
among people who would otherwise never have met them. When,
in the 1860's, a Royal Commission was appointed to examine the
operation of the Penal Servitude Act, and to revise the regulations
made under it, it was to Maconochie's Marks System that it
turned for an alternative.

[1] Webb, S. and B., op. cit.

CHAPTER XIII

TOWARDS A NATIONAL SYSTEM

Little special treatment was accorded to juveniles in the prisons of England at the beginning of the nineteenth century. In 1816, according to du Cane, London prisons alone contained more than three thousand inmates under the age of twenty. Until 1854, when the Reformatory Schools Act empowered courts to send offenders to special reformatories if they were under sixteen years old (after not less than fourteen days in prison), nearly all attempts to provide special conditions for juveniles had been of a voluntary character. Even then, the institutions remained in private hands, although some financial support was given from the Treasury and they were made liable to inspection. In 1857, another Act empowered local authorities to finance the establishment of young people's reformatories, and a special Inspector of Prisons was appointed to devote himself entirely to these institutions.

The earliest step taken by the central government to deal with juveniles more carefully than in a normal prison was made in the Parkhurst Act of 1838. This document observed that it would be to the public advantage if a 'prison' were provided 'in which young Offenders may be detained and corrected, and receive such Discipline as shall appear most conducive to their Reformation and to the Repression of Crime'. An old military hospital at Parkhurst, in the Isle of Wight, was therefore taken over for the confinement of young criminals under the age of eighteen who had been sentenced to transportation. Two clear objects were sought:

1. The penal correction of the offender, by confinement, spare diet, rigorous enforcement of rules, and hard work, so as to deter him from the commission of any future crime, by fear of having to undergo a similar amount of bodily pain and privation;

2. His reformation and instruction in the arts most likely to be useful to him, in the condition of life in which he will find himself placed *on deportation to Australia.*

As seen from the road [wrote Hepworth Dixon, twelve years later], Parkhurst has anything but the appearance of a gaol. More than any other cluster of buildings that we know, it resembles a Moravian settlement. There are two large piles, like the male and female departments of such a community, separated by a narrow valley. One of these wings is set apart for the younger boys – those under fifteen years; in the other are confined those from fifteen to twenty. Between the two piles of buildings stand the cottages of the prison officers; and from the central gates a straight avenue of trees, like those at the entrance of many French and German towns, looks down to the road-side. Lying about the whole, and attached to the prison, is a fine tract of fertile land, about eighty acres in extent: this land the boys have to cultivate and work upon.

. . . You ask to be shown the cells – there are a dozen kinds of them. This has partly arisen from the gaol having been built at intervals, by different people, and sometimes in a very great hurry. There are the ordinary felons' cells in one part – old and very close, dark and otherwise offensive. Nothing could well be worse, or dearer, than these. In the principal wing of the building there is [1850] a range of galleries, with the cells disposed on the plan of Pentonville . . . Then there are, in a separate building, two large, and, as it appears to us, admirable dormitories, in which 158 boys can sleep.

It must be explained, that when a juvenile transported convict is first sent to Parkhurst, he is placed in rigid seclusion for three or four months, as a probationary stage. During this period he . . . is not allowed to speak with, or see, except at chapel, any of his fellow-prisoners; and is instructed in the art of tailoring, or the mystery of knitting stockings. The three or four months of separation is expected to have a painful, and therefore salutary, effect upon his mind: and he is not taken out of it until his good conduct warrants, *or sickness compels it.*

So quickly had the 'Pentonville System' taken root, that it was already, after only eight years, being applied unquestioningly here, upon children, some of whom were not yet adolescent! The Park-hurst Reformatory was abolished after the Reformatory Schools Acts of 1854 and 1857 had been passed, and its buildings were later absorbed into the convict prison system as a penal servitude establishment.

The state prisons (including Parkhurst 'Juvenile Prison') were administered after 1850 by a body of Directors of Convict Prisons, with Sir Joshua Jebb, the architect of Pentonville, as their first chairman. Under the Penal Servitude Act the Directors introduced a Progressive Stage System. This divided sentences into four periods, during which a different type of discipline was applied, the first period being spent in complete isolation. Progress between the stages was marked by the granting of privileges in the way of improved diet, pleasanter labour and distinctive dress. A similar system had been introduced in Ireland by Jebb some years earlier.

The Directors did not hold office for long without incurring severe Parliamentary criticism. A serious increase in crime throughout the country aroused public opinion to demand a further investigation into penal matters, and led to the appoint-ment of a Select Committee of the House of Lords (under the Earl of Carnarvon) upon Prisons and Prison Discipline. This com-mittee was responsible for a strict tightening and drastic re-organization of prison administration, recommended without humanity, and later enshrined in the Prisons Act of 1865.

The Committee proposed that the minimum term of penal servitude should be increased, and that known habitual offenders should be subjected to longer sentences. They objected to Jebb's Progressive System, on the ground that it did not show convicts sufficiently clearly that there was no way of earning remission of time except by industry and good conduct. It further advocated the adoption of Maconochie's Marks System, not only in the state prisons but also in local ones. The Committee insisted upon a general application of cellular isolation throughout the country, as rigorously as possible, 'because it was terrible to criminals'. Only the simplest and most routine drudgery or work was to be given to inmates in their cells, so that instructors of tailoring, mat-making and other trades should no longer have to visit them and thereby 'mitigate the irksomeness of separate confinement'. 'Hard labour, hard fare, and a hard bed' should be imposed upon all inmates of English prisons, no matter what their age or sex, 'to give a more deterrent character to separate imprisonment'. This was a report which contained no trace of humanitarian feeling, and no sign of a desire for reformation of the criminal, as opposed to the wreaking of vengeance upon him. The sympathetic approach of Howard, Elizabeth Fry, Buxton, Maconochie, and the whole procession of philanthropic thinkers who until now had devoted their energies to penal enlightenment, had no influence at all upon the Committee's deliberations.

Immediately the Carnarvon Report was issued, and before its recommendations had been passed into law, the Directors of Convict Prisons proceeded to act upon it. Hammocks were removed from cells, to be replaced by bare wooden beds. The small efforts at educating prisoners in associated classes, which had been made at Pentonville and Millbank, were discontinued, and cells, which had been unlocked during the day, were now kept barred and bolted day and night, and the inmates left in complete and utter isolation.

The 1865 Act proved to be the turning-point in English prison history, for it encroached as far as possible upon the powers still remaining to local government to administer prisons independently, without actually taking away their responsibility. Every prison authority was now definitely required, by the law of the land, to erect separate cells for all prisoners. Any distinction remaining between gaols and houses of correction was abolished, and all inmates, no matter what prison they were confined in, had henceforth to perform penal labour either on the treadmill (first-class labour); or with similar kinds of work, classified as second-class labour, that the Secretary of State might specify. The diets of all prisoners had to conform to Home Office standard. Prison governors were empowered to punish any inmate at their own discretion by close confinement for three days and nights on bread and water, without reference to any superior authority. Visiting Justices were enabled to inflict one whole month in a punishment cell, or a flogging; the use of chains, irons and other methods of mechanical restraint was specifically authorized. However much local circumstances or particular prisoners might differ, a set code of rules, described in the minutest detail, was to be applied everywhere.

This astonishingly severe statute – the more remarkable

H

because it was passed almost without objection by Parliament – contained some valuable innovations. It decreed that from henceforth every prison was to have a doctor and an Anglican chaplain on the staff, and that a coroner's inquest must be held upon every inmate who died in gaol. Furthermore, for the first time, it authorized prison authorities to make some form of grant-in-aid out of public funds to prisoners on discharge.

Thus, in 1865, the basis of a country-wide prison system, with all institutions in it conforming to an acknowledged pattern, was laid. It was laid in a spirit of intolerance and vengeance by men with no insight into the minds of the unfortunate thousands who were to endure it, and who were allowed no chance of rehabilitation.

The best result of the 1865 Act was the closing of many small local prisons. Rather than meet the enormous cost of altering their gaols to comply with the new law, a large number of smaller boroughs gave them up completely, leaving the County Justices responsible for imprisonment. Fourteen institutions had been expressly closed by the Act itself, and the number of prisons in England and Wales dwindled from 193 to 112.

In 1869, a further Act affecting the administration of local prisons was passed. In abolishing sentences on imprisonment for debt, it removed one of the major hindrances the inspectors had been faced with when trying to achieve uniformity. The debtors, to whom arrangements for criminal offenders in prison could not apply, had been a constant difficulty. They could not be restrained from bringing in articles which the others were forbidden; the food, tobacco and other commodities they could have sent to them, were not easily restricted to the debtors' wards.

From 1869 onward, debtors were committed to prison only for contempt of court: for neglecting to make payments to their creditors as ordered by the magistrates. It therefore became possible to subject the smaller number who came to the same discipline as ordinary prisoners, and to apply the uniformity for which Home Office inspectors struggled, to all classes of inmates indiscriminately.[1]

However, it became apparent before long that the desired uniformity in prison administration could not in fact be achieved.

[1] See *Prison Reminiscences*, by 'H' (London, 1859), for an account of the debtors' ward at a local prison in the middle of the nineteenth century.

Building regulations laid down in Whitehall had to be complied with: this was a sphere in which results were tangible. But the attitude of prison staffs could not be changed overnight. The ordinary officer, with the same governor to serve and the same Justices over him as he had before 1865, was not likely, if he had been a lenient man, to turn into an impassive, impatient bully immediately the Act was passed. Severity of treatment still depended to a large degree upon the area in which a criminal happened to be caught, and news of the places which had an 'easy nick' quickly spread among what the Victorians liked to call 'the criminal classes'.

Differences were particularly obvious in the type of labour performed in the institutions. The Home Office stated definitely that no attempt should be made to place goods manufactured by inmates on sale in the open market. This practice, giving governors and Justices a profit incentive, with some relief to local rates, was thought to cause unfair treatment to prisoners and to encourage too much freedom of association among them. Moreover, trade unions were beginning to appear at this time, and to irritate the government. Protests against 'unfair competition' by 'prison labour' might be more easily satisfied than some of their more definitely political claims.

In the state prisons, men and women were employed entirely on work for the government or on tasks which served the prisons themselves. Indeed, the new convict prisons at Chatham and Portland had been established expressly to create a labour supply for excavation and construction work in the royal dockyards. The great mole of Portland harbour, built entirely by the labour of hundreds of convicts, is a permanent memorial to their sufferings. These institutions were paid for directly out of national taxation. But the local prisons were still primarily paid for by the ratepayers, although some proportion of their cost was met by annual grants from the Treasury. Therefore some county prisons continued, in defiance of the Home Office, extremely profitable manufacturing businesses which they had set up before 1865. The former house of correction at Wakefield derived an annual income of over £40,000 from the sale of mats, until after 1877. In some institutions profit-sharing schemes were in operation among the staff, and commercial travellers were employed by them to hawk prison wares to retailers up and down the country. Special bonuses and privileges accorded to inmates who were particularly productive, made nonsense of the Marks System, and did not assist the officers in their attempts to maintain discipline.[1]

Manufacturing for profit was completely abolished by the Prison Commission when it took over absolute control of gaols for the state, but failure to deal with the problem intelligently at that time has left us even today, when it is unanimously agreed that prisoners should be given creative work of value to the community, unable to provide an adequate and steady flow of contracts.

[1] See Clay, W. L., *The Prison Chaplain* (London, 1861), for an account of profitable manufactures at Preston Prison, and Chesterton, G. L., *Revelations of Prison Life* (London, 1856), for a description of similar activities at Coldbath Fields.

CHAPTER XIV

NATIONALIZATION

*'Prison treatment should have as its primary and con-
current objects, deterrence and reformation.'*
The Gladstone Committee, 1895

Aproposal to put all prisons in the country under national
control had been debated and rejected by the Committee
on Prison Discipline in 1850. It was, indeed, a startling
proposal. Never before had a service been transferred entirely, at
one sweep, from local councils to the central government. But in
1874 a government came to power which was pledged to reduce
county rates. It was faced with a striking increase in the number of
men and women committed to prison, and a collection of well
over a hundred separate gaols under local control, nearly all of
them well below the standards of design and administration Parliament had already demanded. To insist that every prison should
be rebuilt or converted to provide cellular accommodation – some
of them to house only fifty inmates or less – would greatly increase the burden borne by local ratepayers. This was politically
impossible.

It was estimated that by closing down the smaller and older
county gaols, £500,000 could be saved. The government's pledge
to ease the county rates could be honoured, and at the same time
the Home Office, as the sole department responsible for prison
administration, could enforce the régime which legally should
already have been practised in gaols throughout the country. All
local objections to uniformity could be removed at a blow: removed in a way which might even be popular with those who had
previously supported them for economic reasons.

The Bill introduced in Parliament in 1876 made it clear that no
dramatic changes in the form of treatment given in prisons was
envisaged. Nevertheless, a Bill intending to put a service entirely
under central control, which had been primarily of local concern
from the earliest times, was bound to meet with some opposition,

chiefly in the national Press. There were charges that such an Act would sap the foundations of the constitutional system, that it represented 'a gigantic and almost unparalleled centralization', and a 'distinct slur upon local government'.[1] It was the carrot of financial relief for their constituents, which, as the government had confidently expected, led the majority of county Members to support the measure in the end. But in its final stages Irish Members (who hoped for some amelioration of the harsh conditions experienced by their countrymen serving sentences for treason) bitterly attacked the Bill.

By the *Prisons Act* of 1877 the Home Secretary was given full Ministerial responsibility for everything concerning the English Prisons. Their ownership and control was vested solely in him, together with all the powers and responsibilities with regard to prisons previously held by local Justices. Subject to the control of the Home Secretary, the general superintendence of the prisons was entrusted to a body of Prison Commissioners, five in number. It was made clear that these gentlemen had no authority but that which derived from the Home Secretary under the Act. They were to be his agents, and he was to answer to Parliament for their decisions. Sir Joshua Jebb's successor as Director-General of Convict Prisons, Sir Edmund du Cane, became the first Chairman of the Prison Commission. For the first time, all local prisons in England and Wales were now subject to a single body of rules, and for the first time the government could make sure that its penal measures were carried out precisely as they were intended to be.

The population of prisoners at this time, in convict and in local institutions, was just over 31,000, larger than it had ever been before. True to the spirit of the Act which had brought them into existence, the Commissioners set to work with economy and efficiency. Of the 112 local prisons placed in their hands on the 1st April 1878, 38 were closed on the very day of transfer. Nineteen more became defunct in the next ten years, and in 1895, when the next national inquiry into prison administration was made (by the Gladstone Committee), the total of convict and local prisons was only 61.

For a decade the Commissioners devoted themselves to bringing order into the variety of organizational methods employed under local government. No two institutions had kept their accounts in

[1] See *Hansard* for 1877.

the same way, the payment and hours of work of the staffs had to be standardized, and an exact routine of work had to be laid down for them. Comparative studies were made as to the effectiveness (as punishments) of different forms of labour applied in the different prisons, and standard diets were worked out for prisoners all over the country. An Inspector of Medical Services was appointed to ensure that even in this department fixed standards were set and recognized in every institution.

Clearly it was necessary at this time for drastic and brutally efficient changes to be introduced. The task of moulding all the different prisons in England and Wales, and every detail of their administration (in which the personalities, prejudices and politics of hundreds of locally employed Justices and governors had been expressed), into one common pattern, was a tremendous one. Prison workers became members of a highly disciplined organization subjected to minute rules covering every aspect of their employment.

Sir Edmund du Cane prided himself on achieving an aim which is the very reverse of that sought in any modern penal institution: the treatment of all offenders exactly alike, with the smallest of variation according to their ages, sex, crimes and social background. The man who entered an English prison under the new order immediately lost all his individuality. He entered a grim, artificial world, where no allowance was made for variations of character and temperament; where any good in him was not recognized, and where all prisoners were considered equally undesirable and wicked. There was a total neglect of the prisoners' minds. The stupid and the intelligent, the skilled and the unskilled, all lost their distinguishing characteristics and suffered equally severe treatment. The English prison system, under du Cane, was a massive machine for the promotion of misery. Ironically, the way in which offenders were treated by the first Prison Commissioners, a method which neither drew out their good qualities nor attempted to instil into them any feelings of moral responsibility or of loyalty to ideas and persons, could only exaggerate the influence of those social and psychological factors which had first made them criminal. But how far can du Cane be held responsible? Parliament had placed the ultimate responsibility for prisons upon the shoulders of the Home Secretary. du Cane was a civil servant, bound to carry out the law without allowing personal feelings to interfere in the cold, rational application of prison rules which Parliament could have changed in a day. All this is true. But a post of such importance as his: a post where the mildest of decisions could affect the mental attitudes and physical well-being of men and women quite unable, while in prison, to direct their own lives, was not one which should be occupied by such a model servant of the government. Humanity is the essential element required of any man in charge of prisoners: a humanity so strong that it will not allow of such a blind, mechanical subservience to a narrow frame of rules as du Cane displayed. The work of a civil servant as lofty in status as du Cane is to question and advise his political master as well as to follow him: to ensure that the politicians are fully aware of the real effects their decisions have.

The du Cane régime was one under which the prisoner slept upon a plank for a bed, worked regularly, tediously and exhaustingly at the crank or the treadmill, and was forced to remain silent, deprived of any social intercourse with other inmates or with the staff, for the whole of his sentence. The profitable industries which some prisons had built up were universally abolished, replaced by tasks which could be performed in isolation in the cells. The crank, the treadmill and the obnoxious and endlessly boring work of oakum picking became the most common forms of work forced upon the prisoner. They were forced upon him no matter how able he was mentally or physically for more constructive tasks. The Prison Commissioners made no attempt to justify their behaviour in terms of reformation and rehabilitation. 'Cellular labour is decidedly brutalizing in its effects', wrote Sir Edmund du Cane. 'To men of any intelligence it is irritating, depressing and debasing to the mental faculties . . .' Alongside the mental torture which his staff were inflicting so rigorously and effectively, du Cane introduced some improvements in sanitary arrangements, which merely throw further stress on the general inhumanity of the system as a whole. Overcrowding was stopped, bathing facilities became available to all prisoners, and hospital accommodation and nursing treatment were improved to a level never before known in prisons anywhere. Thirty thousand men and women were being made to suffer daily, but they were suffering under hygienic conditions.

In instituting their schemes, the first Commissioners were not just putting into practice the ideas of a vengeful, sadistic public Throughout the history of philanthropy, criminals, the people most in need of sympathetic help in their social difficulties, have nearly always been the last to receive it. But the moral indignation felt by the later Victorians toward prisoners was not of a kind which delighted in the infliction of mental and physical cruelty. The du Cane régime, far from following public opinion, was successful in directing it to some extent. Men and women went into prisons as people. They came out as Lombrosian animals, shorn and cropped, hollow-cheeked, and frequently, as a result of dietary deficiencies and lack of sunlight, seriously ill with tuberculosis. They came out mentally numbed and some of them insane; they became the creatures, ugly and brutish in appearance, stupid and resentful in behaviour, unemployable and emotionally unstable, which the Victorian middle classes came to visualize whenever they thought of prisoners. Much of the prejudice against prisoners which remains today may be due to this conception of them not as the commonplace, rather weak people the majority of them really are, but as a composite caricature of the distorted personalities produced by du Cane's machine.

Prison inspectors were instructed to pay attention to the physical structure of prisons and to the inmates' bodily health. Remarks about prisoners' mental suffering rarely appeared in their reports, although occasional comments were made about their passivity and obedience to orders. Among other things, the inspectors had to ensure that cells were kept as clean and devoid of decoration as possible, with opaque glass in the windows so that not even the sky with its changing clouds could be looked at for relief, and that governors did not allow pictures of a prisoner's relatives to remain in his possession.

The Progressive Stage System (an interpretation of Maconochie's scheme) gave inmates some small chance of improving their circumstances by their own efforts. At first a man was put down to 'Hard Labour of the First Class', at least six hours of which had to be on the treadmill or the crank each day. He had no hope of earning any marks toward remission of his sentence at all during this period. Men raised to the second stage (after at least a month from the beginning of a sentence) might be allowed to have school texts in their cells and to take some exercise on a Sunday in the grim circular yard of the prison. In the third stage other small privileges were given. It was not until he had reached the fourth stage of his imprisonment that a man might write and receive letters (at infrequent intervals) and be visited by his parents or his wife in the closely observed visiting-box. This system, with its grudging award of privileges, did not inculcate any sense of responsibility: it made for greater docility, for the passive acceptance of 'institutionalization'. It was applied to people serving very short sentences as well as to the long-term convicts.

At first the du Cane régime appeared to be highly successful. Reports coming from the Commissioners throughout the period from 1877 to 1895 display very considerable self-satisfaction. But these documents provided the only information about current penal methods available to the public: any criticism of the system and any complaint made by an official within the prison service was rigidly suppressed as 'confidential and unsuitable for publication'. The Commissioners could point proudly to the criminal statistics, which showed that the numbers committed to prison had fallen steadily since 1877. But there had been no decrease in recidivism. If the true test of success in penal treatment had been applied; if it had been asked how many of those once released from prison returned again, the work of the Commissioners would have been exposed as a miserable failure. The most blatantly deterrent régime ever instituted in British prisons, a reign of such severity that it was criticized even in Tsarist Russia, had been no more effective in preventing known criminals from falling foul of the law again and again, than had the clumsy, unco-ordinated prisons of the years before 1877. After subjection to the new form of treatment, prisoners were even less able to deal with the common obligations of ordinary life than they had been before. They were so drilled in silent obedience, so docile, so accustomed to aimless labour, and so unused to situations calling for thought on their part, that freedom itself was a burden to them.

Slowly, as scraps of information about life in the prisons escaped through official barriers, public indignation at its inhumanity began to awaken. It reached full flood after du Cane's dismissal of a prison chaplain who had ignored the censorship and had written a newspaper article criticizing the Prison Commissioners. This action brought sweeping condemnation of the whole prison administration in a Press campaign organized by the minister con-

cerned, the Rev. W. D. Morrison, to defend himself. The Gladstone Committee gives a highly restrained account of the campaign: 'In brief, not only were the principles of prison treatment
as prescribed by the Prison Acts criticized, but the prison authority itself, and the constitution of that authority, were held to be
responsible for many grave evils that were said to exist.' Asquith,
who became Home Secretary in the Liberal Government of 1892,
could not hold out against the storm of protest aroused by Morrison's revelations. In 1894 he set up a Departmental Committee
with the Under-Secretary of State (later Lord Gladstone) as its
chairman, to examine the accusations. 'The moral condition in
which a large number of prisoners leave the prison, and the serious
number of recommittals', announced a Home Office report,
'have led us to think that there is ample cause for a searching inquiry into the main features of prison life.'

The Gladstone Committee were given terms of reference which
would exclude them from commenting upon penal principles and
upon the way in which the Prison Commissioners had sought to
put them into practice. They found it impossible to recognize such
limitations, and ignored them entirely in making their recommendations. The conclusions they came to were a serious indict-
ment of the entire du Cane régime and of the penal ideas it
expressed.

> We think [reported the Committee] that the system should
> be made more elastic, more capable of being adapted to the
> special cases of individual prisoners; that prison discipline
> should be more effectually designed to maintain, stimulate or
> awaken the higher susceptibilities of prisoners, to develop
> their moral instincts, to train them in orderly and industrious
> habits, and whenever possible, to turn them out of prison
> better men and women physically and morally than when
> they came in.

du Cane's main achievement, the chief source of his pride,
uniformity of treatment, was roundly condemned. Prisoners had
been treated too much as 'a hopeless or worthless element of the
community' and 'the moral as well as the legal responsibility of
the prison authorities' had been too easily regarded as finished
once the prisoners had passed through the gates on discharge.

All the energies of the despotic, ageing du Cane were now

declared misdirected; but the blame for his prison administration was not directly laid upon his shoulders or upon those of the Commissioners as a whole, who, said the Report,

> have carried into effect under successive Secretaries of State the Acts approved by Parliament; who have loyally and substantially carried out the various recommendations made from time to time by Commissions and Committees; and who, as administrators, have achieved in point of organization, discipline, order, and economy, a striking administrative success.

> But under this orderly equality [continued the Report] there exist the most striking inequalities. The hardened criminal bears the discipline without much trouble. Others are brutalized by it. Others suffer acutely and perhaps are permanently weakened by it in mind and body. What is a temporary inconvenience to the grown criminal, may be to lads and younger men a bitter disgrace from which they never recover to their dying day. It is impossible to administer to each man a relatively exact amount of punishment. But yet it is these very inequalities which often must produce that bitterness and recklessness which lead on to habitual crime.

The Committee was considerably influenced in its findings by the testimony of Sir Godfrey Lushington, who, as Permanent Under-Secretary, was one of the most influential men in the Home Office.

> I regard as unfavourable to reformation the status of a prisoner throughout his whole career [he said], the crushing of self-respect; the starving of all moral instinct he may possess; the absence of all opportunity to do or receive a kindness; the continual association with none but criminals, and that only as a separate item among other items also separate; the forced labour and the denial of liberty. I believe the true mode of reforming a man, or restoring him to society, is exactly in the opposite direction of all these.

The Committee was firmly opposed to the idea of deterrence by excessive severity. It advised that all 'penal labour', such as the treadmill and the crank, should be abolished, and again, in dramatic reversal of du Cane's policy, recommended that productive labour should be reintroduced, not as a means of making money, but because of the good effect it would have upon prisoners. The solid basis of prison discipline as it was then known, cellular confinement, was itself criticized. As applied in the first stage of penal servitude, the Committee described it as a terrible ordeal, the length of which should be carefully reconsidered.

Sir Evelyn Ruggles-Brise, du Cane's successor as Chairman of the Prison Commission, wrote:

> The public enquiry of 1894 into prison administration was a practical condemnation of the separate or cellular system, except for short periods. It swept aside the old-fashioned idea that separate confinement was desirable on the ground that it enables the prisoner to meditate on his misdeeds. It held that association for industrial labour under proper conditions should be productive of no harm.[1]

The Committee's Report was accepted by the government of the day in its entirety. Fortunately, du Cane was about to retire when it was issued, and without undue embarrassment Asquith was able to appoint Ruggles-Brise to succeed him. The new Chairman had the responsibility of putting the Committee's recommendations into practice. But the work which du Cane had achieved so swiftly could be reformed less speedily. It was not until 1898 that a new Act of Parliament incorporating most of the desired changes was passed.

In 1910 it was still possible for a well-informed writer on penal matters[2] to observe that

> If we look for the really essential changes during a hundred years we find just these:
> (1) A surface cleanliness of apparent perfection;
> (2) Conversation, prison visits and arrangements tending towards a decent sociability between prisoners and prisoners, and between prisoners and the public, reduced and rendered difficult by multitudinous byelaws.

But this judgement, which would have been a fair one if made upon the du Cane régime, was not true of the spirit in which the

[1] Ruggles-Brise, Sir Evelyn, *The English Prison System* (London, 1921).
[2] Murison, A. F., Introduction to *The Criminal and the Community*, by Devon, J. (London, 1910).

Commissioners were now setting about their task. While Murison was writing, a great loosening process was under way in British prisons: a gradual abolition of the fierce deterrent practices, and a gradual introduction of definitely reformative methods.

The 1898 Act introduced remission of sentences, where they exceeded a month, by one-sixth of their length (conditional upon good behaviour). 'First Class Hard Labour' was abolished completely. Corporal punishment was limited to offences of mutiny, gross personal violence to a prison official, or incitement to mutiny, and a system was introduced whereby men committed to prison in default of a fine could buy their release on part payment of it. The Home Secretary was empowered to make any changes in the system by Parliamentary Rule, without recourse to a new Act.

CHAPTER XV

A FRESH DESIGN

'It is certain that the ages when the majority of habitual criminals are made, lie between 16 and 21 . . . the most fatal years are 17, 18 and 19.'

Gladstone Committee, 1895

Sir Edmund du Cane left one permanent memorial behind him: Wormwood Scrubs Prison, which was built by prison labour from Millbank between 1874 and 1890. It departed from the Pentonville plan only in that its cellular halls were isolated from one another in separate blocks, not linked together in a radial pattern. Originally, Wormwood Scrubs had been intended to take first offenders who had not previously been in prison: it was, and is, the largest penitentiary in Britain, with accommodation in separate cells for over 1,400 inmates. Here at Ducane Road is the cenotaph of penal repression, a mass of stone which even now, by its very shape, hinders the reformative work which we are attempting to do.

Until 1908 there was no separate provision of any kind in our system for offenders between 16 and 21 years. The trend in the twentieth century has been to reduce the prison population by using more and more alternative means of treatment, determined by the age, offences and background of the delinquents concerned. Within the prison system repeated efforts have been made to vary the character of the institutions and the types of training practised in them. The first step towards this great process of differentiation applied to young offenders.

Long before he became directly involved in prison administration, Sir Alexander Paterson visited a youth who was confined in Dartmoor. His record of Dartmoor Prison in 1906, where a boy of under 21 had been sent, shows how slowly the reforms stimulated by the Gladstone Committee were taking effect, and how great was the need for a new kind of institution serving young criminals:

As I walked along the endless landings and corridors in the great cellular blocks, I saw something of the fifteen hundred men who were then immured in Dartmoor. Their drab uniforms were plastered with broad arrows,[1] their heads were closely shaven, which might make them of interest to the phrenologist but would have baffled any portrait painter. Not even a safety razor was allowed, so that in addition to the stubble on their heads, their faces were covered with a sort of dirty moss, representing the growth of hair that a pair of clippers could not remove. The prison régime, resting primarily on conditions of safe custody and security, determined to minimize the chances of violence or suicide, had succeeded in making a large number of human beings into objects of ugliness and contempt. No child could have recognized his father in such conditions, no girl or wife believe she ever loved a man who looked like that. As they saw us coming, each man ran to the nearest wall and put his face closely against it, remaining in this servile position until we had passed behind him. This was a strictly ordered procedure, to avoid assault or familiarity, the two great offences in prison conduct, the relative gravity of which no one has ever assessed.

The men looked hard in body and spirit, healthy enough in physique and colour, but cowed and listless in demeanour and response. No active brutality was practised by the warders, save when an escaped convict was recaptured. Then it was the age-long tradition of the place that he should be taken down to a separate cell and beaten indiscriminately. This practice is common in most prisons in the world, but is not now extant in this country. Otherwise, the only occasions of violence were the fights amongst the convicts, which occurred weekly.

It would be difficult to exaggerate the depravity and degradation of life to which these men sank in those days. Their language cannot be printed, their habits cannot be

[1] The broad arrow disappeared from prisoners' clothing shortly after the First World War.

Strangeways Prison, Manchester, 1948, showing tiered cells. A typical example of 'Pentonville' type prison, post 1850

described. Any man who came from a decent home outside
was appalled to discover that men could fall to such depths of
immoral beastliness, and the average man was inevitably
dragged down by the conduct and example of the men around
him, whose company he could not escape. Within a year, he
was almost unrecognizable in speech and habit and point of
view.[1]

Slow as the Prison Commissioners were to change conditions
like these, their new Chairman, Sir Evelyn Ruggles-Brise, was
responsible for one of the most drastic innovations in modern
penal history: the Borstal System. Following upon the concern of
the Gladstone Committee for 'the rescue of young offenders', who
'under the present system, come out of prison in a condition as
bad or worse than that in which they came', he himself visited the
United States to study the Elmira State Reformatory, an institution for men between 16 and 30 years old.

I was impressed by all that I saw and learnt at the principal
State Reformatories of America [wrote Ruggles-Brise]. The
elaborate system of moral, physical and industrial training of
these prisoners, the enthusiasm which dominated the work,
the elaborate machinery for supervision of parole, all these
things, if stripped of their extravagances, satisfied me that a
real, human effort was being made in these States for the
rehabilitation of the youthful criminal. It was on my return
that the first experiments were begun of the special treatment,
with a view to the rehabilitation of the young prisoners,
16 to 21, in London Prisons.

An association was formed of men prepared to visit these
youths and take a special individual interest in them. These voluntary workers went in each month according to a rota, to interview the lads and make some arrangements for their welfare after
discharge. They were the originals of the Borstal Association
which today, with more definite functions, is the most nearly
satisfactory arrangement we have for the after-care of any class of
convicted offender. In its early days the association depended upon
a Treasury grant of only £100, and upon a few small voluntary
subscriptions.

[1] Quoted in the Introduction, by Ruck, S. K., to *Paterson on Prisons* (London, Frederick Muller, 1951).

I

The object of the system now established by Ruggles-Brise was 'to arrest or check the evil habit by the "individualization" of the prisoner, mentally, morally and physically'. A prison in the Kentish village of Borstal (which had been used previously as a satellite of Chatham convict prison) was taken over, and there, with a carefully selected staff, gymnastics, formal educational classes and 'inducements to good conduct by a system of grades and rewards' were introduced, 'to encourage a spirit of healthy emulation and inspire self-respect'. Special rules applying to this new institution were introduced, but there was no formal statutory recognition of the scheme by Parliament, and consequently all the young men dealt with were transferred from other prisons, often serving quite short sentences.

> It soon became clear that the element of time, that is, a longer sentence than the law permitted, was essential for the success of the scheme. Experience showed . . . that the system should be one of stern and exact discipline, tempered only by such rewards and privileges as good conduct, with industry, might earn: and resting on its physical side on the basis of hard manual labour . . .
>
> [The sentence] should not be less than three years, conditional liberation being freely granted, when the circumstances of any case gave a reasonable prospect of reclamation, and when the Borstal Association, after careful study of the case, felt able to make fair provision on discharge.[1]

In 1906, after four years' experiment at Borstal, Ruggles-Brise made representations to the Home Secretary, requesting a change in the law to enable the new scheme to become an established and recognized way of dealing with both males and females between the ages of 16 and 21. Borstal treatment was legally instituted in 1908, under the *Prevention of Crimes Act*.

Where 'criminal habit and tendency or association was proved' the courts were now empowered to impose detention for any length of time up to three years in a state reformatory known as a 'Borstal Institution'. Thus, power was given to the staffs of the institutions to determine the precise length of time served by individual inmates, and the youths were given the most powerful of incentives to co-operate in the training given to them. The

[1] Ruggles-Brise, op. cit.

distinguishing characteristic of Borstal training from the very beginning was its stress, not on the docility of the prisoner and the ease with which he conformed to orders, but upon the capacity and willingness he showed to live an orderly, law-abiding life after discharge. At last it was formally recognized that the forcing of human beings to behave like placid automata was not the best way of preparing them to resist criminal temptations.

Today, there are over twenty Borstal Institutions, but the atmosphere which pervades them is due to Sir Alexander Paterson rather than to their founder, Ruggles-Brise. At first, however unlike the prisons they were, they still bore some mark of severity. It was Paterson's remarkable enthusiasm and vitality, communicating itself to all the men who met him, which made the task 'not to break the Borstal lad or knead him into shape, but to stimulate some power within to regulate conduct aright, to *insinuate* a preference for the good and the clean, to make him want to use his life well, so that he himself and not others will save him from waste'.[1]

At about the time when the Borstal System, our most enlightened contribution to international penal methods, became established, two other Acts of Parliament, the *Probation of Offenders Act* (1907) and the *Children Act* (1908), further reduced the scope of imprisonment.

The Probation Act had its origins in the *Summary Jurisdiction Act* of 1879 and in the *Probation of First Offenders Act* of 1887, which had given the courts power to discharge offenders in trifling cases, or in circumstances where the youth, character and background of a person convicted of larceny or of false pretences for the first time, justified it. He could be released immediately, and made liable to be called up for judgement only if he failed to be of good behaviour.

Voluntary social workers (in particular the Church of England Temperance Society) had proved that by befriending and advising offenders of this type they could often keep them from committing further crimes and help them to solve their personal social difficulties.

Courts were now empowered to appoint their own Probation Officers to continue and develop this work. A prisoner could be given the choice of accepting supervision by an Officer instead of serving a more conventional sentence. In this way the treatment

---

[1] Paterson, A., *Principles of the Borstal System* (London, 1932).

method which has proved in the long run to be by far the most successful in our penal system was introduced. But many magistrates' courts were very nervous of their new powers. In 1909 the number of probation orders made was only 9,000. At the outbreak of war in 1914, just over 11,000 orders were being made annually. The Departmental Committee on The Training of Probation Officers had to report in 1922 that a quarter of the magistrates' courts in England and Wales were still without a Probation Officer. The *Criminal Justice Act* of 1925 bound all police courts to make such an appointment. Since then the probation service has had a steady and continuous growth, affording positive and constructive help to men, women and young people who would otherwise have been subjected to a less definitely rehabilitative form of treatment, and extending its influence well into the field of after-care. The success of the probation service is due very largely to the quality of the men and women who have been attracted to work in it, to the excellence of their training[1] (which is more thorough and more enlightened than that usually given even to the most senior officials in the Prison Service) and to the fact that probation work is carried out in the offender's own environment, where the social factors influencing him can often be seen and interpreted by the Officer, although they cannot be easily modified by him.

The *Children Act* of 1908 prohibited the imprisonment of any person under the age of 16, except in very special circumstances. It also introduced a classification of under-fourteen-year-olds as 'children', and of those between 14 and 16 as 'young persons'. Children were not to be put into prison under any circumstances in the future. The Act also introduced special juvenile courts: cases involving children were to be heard privately and in a different place from the adult court. (The *Children and Young Persons Act* of 1933 made the new courts more effective by restricting the magistrates allowed to sit in them to those who had special experience or knowledge of children.[2])

One further Act promised to reduce the range of people who could be committed to prison, before the outbreak of war in 1914 called a temporary halt to the progress of penal reform. The

[1] Substantial numbers of untrained men and women have been accepted into the service since the war. Special 'in service' training schemes are being organized for them, but it may be that only generic case-work training is really of maximum value.

[2] One of the magistrates in a juvenile court is always a woman.

Mental Deficiency Act of 1913 required the removal of mental defectives, who would hitherto have been confined in prison, to a state institution or to a normal mental hospital.

These measures, as they took effect, put the English prison system, as far as legal provision was concerned, virtually in the condition which still prevailed at the time of the *Criminal Justice Act* of 1948. But in the thirty years after the end of the First World War great changes took place in the administration of the system, and particularly in the attitude with which prison staffs faced their enormous responsibility. If the English prisons became, during that time, more effective in their true purpose of social rehabilitation, and more humane, it was due not so much to formal Parliamentary decisions or to the enforcement of new rules by the Home Secretary, as to the increasingly sympathetic approach of the men and women working in them.

The *Prevention of Crime Act* which had introduced the Borstal System in 1908 also created a new form of imprisonment. It had become clear that 'professional' criminals were not deterred by successive sentences of a conventional kind, or by penal servitude. Courts were therefore empowered to award (to 'habitual' criminals only) a period of from five to ten years' preventive detention in addition to penal servitude. An habitual criminal was defined as a person who came up for trial after having had no less than three previous convictions since the age of 16, and who could be shown to have made no effort to lead an honest life since last released from prison. In acknowledgement of the principle (a new one in English penology) that the sentence was for the protection of the public rather than for the punishment of the criminal, a principle which aimed to prevent quite as much as to deter or to reform, convicts subjected to this Act were allowed extra comforts on completing the first (or penal servitude) period. A special prison, at Camp Hill near Parkhurst in the Isle of Wight, was built especially to take the Preventive Detainees. It was one of the last buildings to be erected in this country specifically for use as a prison, until the completion of Everthorpe Hall (near Hull) in 1958.[1]

[1] Nottingham and Norwich prisons were built in the first years of this century. Everthorpe Hall was intended as a maximum security prison, but owing to the pressure on Borstal accommodation it has been used as a Borstal institution since it was opened. Another maximum security institution is now in process of construction at Hindley, near Wigan.

The system instituted at Camp Hill was considerably less severe than penal servitude, but the idea of inflicting two sentences for one offence was new to the traditions of English law, and the courts did not welcome preventive detention. The numbers committed to the new prison did not, in the end, justify the reservation of one institution, the newest in the prison system, solely for this special type of convict. The Webbs wrote, in 1922:

> We suspect that it passes the wit of man to contrive a prison which shall not be gravely injurious to the minds of the vast majority of the prisoners, if not also to their bodies. So far as can be seen at present, the most practical and hopeful of 'prison reforms' is to keep people out of prison altogether! It is in this direction that the present Prison Commissioners, and the Home Office, have been, during the last two decades, making most progress.[1]

The Webbs did not foresee the large-scale development of 'open prisons' which has taken place in this country since the nineteen-twenties, or the appointment to the Prison Commission of as lively and imaginative a man as Alexander Paterson.

Sir Evelyn Ruggles-Brise retired from the Chairmanship of the Prison Commission in 1921. His reign had not been a dramatic one, but under him the prison service, and the way in which it interpreted criminal statutes, had not entirely lagged behind the ambitions of positive reformers. Those ambitions had not always been opposed, and, indeed, every innovation made by the Prison Commissioners had been one of hopeful and unsentimental improvement.

Sir Evelyn had been deputy to du Cane in the last years of his régime: a deputy conscientiously carrying out his duties as an established civil servant, but with inward disagreement with much of du Cane's rigorous interpretation of the law. We are told how, shortly after his arrival as du Cane's assistant, Ruggles-Brise expressed mild disapproval of one small point of policy, whereupon his chief never spoke to him again, conducting all business between them by means of subordinates. After Morrison's allegations about the du Cane régime had been heard, it was the carefully phrased but courageous evidence of Sir Evelyn Ruggles-

[1] Webb, S. and B., op. cit.

Brise which most strongly influenced the Gladstone Committee. This was a balanced summary made by a man who definitely sought more humane legislation and did not hesitate to indicate where he thought improvements were necessary in the prison service and how they should be carried out.

During the Ruggles-Brise administration English prisons saw the arrival of suffragettes and of conscientious objectors, most of them literate, well-educated people who were able to express their feelings of injustice in a way which attracted public attention. Their writings added to the fund of informed interest about life within prison walls, which was now growing among ordinary men and women. For many who have since risen to literary and political eminence, the experience of imprisonment at this time began a life-long interest in penal reform and in the welfare of ex-prisoners.

Sir (then Mr) Maurice Waller succeeded Sir Evelyn as Chairman, and at the same time Alexander Paterson was appointed a member of the Prison Commission. Together they introduced some radical changes, the most symbolic and immediately apparent of which were the abolition of the convict 'crop' and the 'broad arrow' which had for long been a mark of shame and which now, forty years afterwards, still serve to indicate a prisoner in newspaper cartoons. Prison Visitors were introduced for male as well as female prisoners, and new clothing was designed for inmates. In a few prisons visits were allowed to take place in a relaxed way, across an ordinary table, instead of in degrading wire-netted boxes.[1]

Paterson, whose interest in penology had been first aroused by contact with a young murderer at an East End boys' club, who had been shocked by Dartmoor at the turn of the century, and who had been an enthusiastic participant in the first Borstal experiments, was now to impress a deeper mark upon prison discipline than any of his predecessors. He did not accept the Chairmanship of the Prison Commission when Sir Maurice Waller retired in 1928, preferring instead to regard himself as 'a missionary, rather than an administrator'. He was determined to retain the freedom he always exercised so effectively, to encourage and inspire, and, where necessary, to convert to his ideas, the men and women who

---

[1] But the wire-netted box, cutting the prisoner off from his visitor almost completely, has by no means disappeared from English prisons even today.

worked in prisons and Borstals. He showed that it was possible for prison work to be regarded truly as a social service, giving treatment, instead of as a routine, repressive, and unpleasant series of tasks performed in daily ritual. He had the power to instil into the governors, officers and other staff he met, a genuine feeling of pride in activity which could now be creative: which could now become a service of *giving* to others, not of depriving them. Paterson drew into the Prison Service men from less hidden walks of life, imbuing them with some of his own powerful dedication, and making them feel that in prisons they could, instead of confining criminals with rigid discipline, awaken in them a new sense of freedom: orderly freedom, to be lived afresh, one day, outside the high thick walls.

Paterson's influence was particularly strong in the Borstal System, which now took on a new, invigorated aspect. By 1930 there were still only three Borstals for boys, and one, at Aylesbury, for girls. They still wore the appearance of prisons. Two of them, at Rochester and Portland, were in converted prison buildings, and a third, at Feltham,[1] in an old industrial school with long cellular halls little different from those of Wormwood Scrubs. In that year came the great change inspired by Paterson's dictum that 'you cannot train men for freedom in a condition of captivity'. A large group of boys selected from Feltham Institution marched the 132 miles to Lowdham Grange, near Nottingham.

> There were no guards, no uniforms, nothing to distinguish the company from any boys' club on the hike. . . . One of the staff who was on that journey once characterized it as an act of faith, which indeed it was. There was no previous experience by which it was possible to judge the chances of success or the chances that the boys might break away or misbehave. But it passed without incident. The boys at first lived in tents or huts while they levelled the ground and built their own institution, which is now a harmonious and dignified group of buildings in the midst of its own gardens and farm lands, with no high wall or barbed wire to cut it off from the surrounding countryside. And so we got our first open Borstal.[2]

[1] All of these are still in use today.
[2] *Borstal, a Critical Survey*, by Elkin, W. A., and Kittermaster, D. B. (London, The Howard League for Penal Reform, 1952).

At Lowdham Grange there are no physical barriers to escape: it is purely the inmate's sense of responsibility, to the development of which the whole training is directed, which causes him to remain within the boundaries. It is the oldest of many 'Open Borstals' in use today; it was the first experiment in a type of institution which has now become almost commonplace. We still have Borstals in old convict prisons: Reading Gaol, proudly built in 1845, the gaol which inspired Oscar Wilde's *Ballad* before the century began, is in use as a Borstal Institution in 1959. But a Borstal may now be a dignified country house or a collection of simple wooden huts.

In 1934 the first 'open prison' was introduced in England, at New Hall Camp, near Wakefield. It is used today just as it was then, as a satellite of the large prison at Wakefield, from which selected men serving long sentences are taken for the last stage of their imprisonment.[1] It is a place where they can work in the open air on a farm, instead of in the dim, closed workshops of a normal institution. It is a place where they can maintain some contact with the free world, and enjoy a less formal relationship (and more revealing association) with the staff than can ever be possible in the ordinary prisons we know. There are now fourteen open prisons in England, all but two of them independent, with their own governing staff and officers living in houses intermixed with the more official buildings. From these places, parties of prisoners may go out each day to work (sometimes alongside ordinary civilian labour) on local farms or in local factories. To an even greater degree than in the closed prisons of today, members of the public may visit them, by invitation, to see plays produced by the inmates or to look at exhibitions of their work. Schoolmasters and other professional men may come in to lecture, or to take part in 'brains trusts' or 'Any Questions' programmes, and local sporting teams play games against prison sides.

The open prisons all met with considerable opposition from the local people when they were first proposed. Always there has been a fear that criminals put down in the countryside near homes and businesses would come and go as they pleased, stealing property and violating the law in countless ways. And always, after the institutions have become established, these fears have slowly been

---

[1] But it is shortly to be given over for use as a Detention Centre for young offenders.

replaced by interest in them, and even affection for them. In July 1958, Mr Percy Wells, the local Member of Parliament, was able to recall, when opening a public exhibition at Eastchurch, the largest of our open prisons, that he had been asked, eight years previously, when that prison was first instituted, to lead a deputation of protest to the Home Office. Now he could, instead, pay tribute to the many ways in which the people of the neighbouring village assisted the governor and his staff in their work.

The new policy practised after the appointment of Sir Maurice Waller was well expressed in the Report of the Prison Commissioners for 1925:

> It is the policy of the administration to carry out its duty of protecting society by training offenders, as far as possible, for citizenship; and every change in the prison system is directed to that end. Prisons exist to protect society, and they can only give efficient protection in one of two ways, either:
>
> (*a*) by removing the anti-social person from the community altogether or for a long period; or
> (*b*) by bringing about some change in him.

Any general application of the first method would not be supported by public opinion. The prison administration must therefore do its utmost to apply the second; that is to say, to restore the man who has been imprisoned to ordinary standards of citizenship, so far as this can be done within the limits of his sentence. Unless some use can be made of the period of imprisonment to change the anti-social outlook of the offender and to bring him into a more healthy frame of mind towards his fellow-citizens, he will, on leaving the prison gates after a few weeks or months, again become a danger, or at any rate a nuisance. He may, indeed, be worse than before, if the only result has been to add a vindictive desire for revenge on society to the selfish carelessness of the rights of others which he brought into prison with him . . .

Thus the function of the twentieth-century prison was recognized as one of education: of changing a man's outlook and behaviour persuasively, not violently. We are still in the slow, grinding process of transforming our prisons into places where this work may be performed smoothly and effectively. The process has brought on to some prison staffs a variety of new creatures: psychologists, psychiatrists, social workers, welfare officers and tutor organizers (education officers), still, sometimes, rather warily regarded by well-established older members of the Prison Service who are accustomed to traditional methods and are uncertain of the value of specialist techniques.

The aim of the modern prison system is stated simply in Rule 6 of the rules published in accordance with the *Criminal Justice Act* of 1948. It is a rule deeply ingrained into the minds of men and women of the prison service, no matter what their grade, almost from the very day they join it:

> The purpose of training and treatment of convicted prisoners shall be to establish in them the will to lead a good and useful life on discharge, and to fit them so to do.

It cannot be claimed that we have a system for carrying out that purpose which even approaches perfection. But here is the modern object of imprisonment in England, clearly stated. Although we have a prison population larger than that at any time since 1900, the object is being pursued more wholeheartedly and enthusiastically than any earlier policy.

PART TWO

Our Prisons Today and in the Future

'*As criminals can neither be coerced nor bribed into a change of purpose, there is but one way left: they must be educated. We must provide a training which will make them, not good prisoners, but good citizens; a training which will fit them for the free life to which, sooner or later, they are to return . . . they should be educated, not for the life inside, but for the life outside. Not until we think of our prisons as educational institutions shall we come within sight of a successful system; and by a successful system I mean, one that not only ensures a quiet, well-behaved prison, but has* genuine life in it as well; *one that restores to society the largest number of intelligent, forceful, honest citizens.*'

THOMAS MOTT OSBORNE
Prisons and Commonsense, 1924

CHAPTER XVI

THE PROBLEMS OF TODAY

Our prisons are imperfect. The law now states that they shall reform the men committed to them, and the Prison Commissioners are devoted to this object, but still a large army of recidivists comes back to their gates again and again. Some part of our community still wants prisons to be instruments of punishment, and punishment alone, so that one experience of them shall deter a criminal from ever committing crimes again.[1] The lessons of the nineteenth century have not been learned by all of us, and the Prison Commissioners have to struggle against loudly advocated punitive policies as well as against general public apathy, in its efforts to rehabilitate criminals. Even flogging still has its adherents. Few men and women who have experienced imprisonment today, even in an open institution, would relish the prospect of going through that experience again. But a high percentage of recidivists seriously inadequate in personality cannot help returning, despite themselves. They may need some sort of semi-institutional help, with periodic 'holidays' outside, for most of their lives. These are people 'institutionalized' by their past experience of imprisonment: people who find inside prison a sense of security and order they cannot achieve independently. The Prison Commissioners are determined to prevent such institutionalization in the future, as far as they possibly can.

The only penal policy we can follow in the future is one of positive rehabilitation. But how can criminals be reformed? Until we can answer this question our prison system cannot even approach perfection. It is really a large number of questions combined into one, for we can be certain that the factors leading men into crime are very varied indeed. A mere glance at the problem makes one long for the certainty with which humanitarians of

---

[1] One weakness of this argument is, of course, that by no means all criminals are caught by the police, and the 'pain' of imprisonment does not inevitably follow the 'pleasure' of committing crime.

the nineteenth century professed that poverty was the cause of crime: that if poverty were abolished, acquisitive offences, at least, would virtually disappear. Today, with a wider distribution of the national wealth than has ever existed before; when genuine poverty is virtually non-existent, the number of crimes known to the police rises steadily each year.

Crime is our greatest single social problem. It is also, tragically, the problem to which sociologists have been able to give least attention. The University of London (at the London School of Economics[1]) has devoted a small part of its resources to criminological research for many years, but it was not until 1958 that sufficient official support and sufficient money were forthcoming for an Institute of Criminology to be established at Cambridge. It is from this institute and from the sociological and psychological research departments of other universities that a knowledge of the true causes of criminal behaviour must eventually come. But it will be many years before we can claim that even a small part of this knowledge is ours. In the meantime, we must ensure that the Prison Service has sufficient money, sufficient buildings of the right design, and staff of sufficient training to make the best attempt at rehabilitative work now possible. That we should do this to protect ourselves from theft, assault, or any other kind of criminal act which might be committed against us, is obvious. We should also do it for the sake of those our society has made and is making into criminals. The criminal varies in appearance and manner as widely as any cross-section of the normal population. He is no more nor less intelligent, no more nor less good-looking than we are, but like the mentally ill he usually experiences much inward suffering.[2]

A criminal act may or may not be an unconscious act of hostility against society and its conventions. The man who commits it is almost certainly one who cannot lead a fully satisfying life, adequately expressing his personality. He is a man in need of treatment: of psychiatric or medical attention or guidance into new fields of work and opportunity where he can be in harmony with conventions of behaviour we all accept. Can we then liken

[1] And now also at University College.
[2] Unless really deficient in super ego, when it is hard for him to give up crime because it brings inward satisfaction. In this case, the exchange is often neurosis.

Mail-bag making at Strangeways Prison, Manchester

a prison to a hospital? The prisons of today sadly resemble hospitals in which the few proven methods of treatment available are applied only to a small proportion of the patients who need them, and even then are applied by unqualified physicians. It is almost unbelievable that in 1959 the majority of the English prisons should have not a single psychologist on their staffs, nor anyone who has had any formal training in the social sciences.

PRISON BUILDINGS

The most immediate problem facing our prisons today is that posed by the buildings they are contained in. As we have seen, all but four were built before the twentieth century, in times when the aim was to oppress the prisoner. But new methods of treatment can only be used properly in buildings designed especially for the purpose. None of our existing 'closed' prisons (and here I include Everthorpe Hall) is suitable for the practice of really modern therapeutic methods. None of them, despite the introduction of bright paint and Marley tiles, is a place which by its very shape and internal arrangement helps prisoners to overcome their resentment and regain their self-respect. The internal arrangement of a building can influence the degree and quality of personal relationships within it to a remarkable degree. These relationships will not develop healthily in huge, impersonal blocks of cells where the individual is dwarfed by the overpowering size of the structure. They can only be attempted in buildings which respect the quality of the individual by being attractive, as normal in appearance as possible, and suitable in scale. Prison design has always lagged behind the most advanced penal thinking of the time, but there is no reason why this should be so in the future, if designers in each country are prepared to profit by one another's experiments and mistakes. Since Pentonville was erected, the United States of America and the Scandinavian countries have seen a whole range of experimental buildings, all of them more closely related to contemporary methods than any prisons we possess. Yet The Times[1] commented upon our newest prison building, Everthorpe:

> Even more remarkable than the innovations is the evidence of how little the basic design of a prison has altered in a

[1] 29 May 1959.

K

century. Here are still the familiar double blocks . . . above
all, here are the usual open halls. They may not be so daunt-
ingly tall, but the idea is the same as in every prison since
Pentonville, when isolation rather than training was the chief
demand. . . .

The author of the article goes on to comment that the perimeter
wall alone at Everthorpe, which is eighteen feet high and was
erected at a cost of £65,000 (or 10 per cent. of the total expenditure on the building) has already been scaled by the Borstal boys
at present held there. But why must a wall be erected round a
modern prison? The number of 'escape risks' among prisoners is
not really large. All the men who are so dangerous to the public
that they must have a thick high wall around them[1] can be
accommodated in a small part of one institution. Nothing more
than a wire fence is really necessary on the boundaries of most
of our prisons.

The objection to walls such as those put up at Everthorpe is
not made on grounds of economy alone. The grave matter is
that so long as penal institutions are made to look like impregnable
fortresses their staffs will tend to adopt a 'fortress psychology'.
The prison fortresses of England create for their administrators problems which are quite separate from the essential task
of reformative training. There is so great a concentration on
'security', on the continual locking and unlocking of doors and
gates, on counting and recounting heads to make sure that no
one has 'gone over' (and it is pitifully easy for a determined
prisoner to get over the walls of any of our prisons, despite all
the precautions), that the real purpose of the institution is pushed
into a secondary place.

The shape of the prisons we now use is not their only defect.
They are housing far too many men. Most local institutions
contain more than 200 men, many nearly a thousand, and two,
Wormwood Scrubs and Wandsworth, have a population of well
over a thousand. Inevitably these institutions contain many
different types of offender, of various ages and sentences, with
often no proper segregation and no opportunity for classification
and training. Any new prisons we build should either be very
much smaller than those we have now, or composed of a number

---

[1] Including psychopaths and those with distinct psychopathic traits.

of small, virtually independent units in which individual treatment is possible and true segregation of different types of inmate
can be achieved. The future of prison design will be commented
upon in the final chapter.

THE PROBLEM OF WORK

It is proving increasingly difficult for the Prison Commissioners
to provide work for prisoners. The demand for mailbags, the
traditional product of prison industry, has fallen, while the
number of men committed to prisons has increased. Many inmates
are now occupied in other, equally monotonous tasks, such as
dismantling telephone equipment.

The work given to men in prison should be of a character that
will not interfere with the definitely rehabilitative aspects of their
training, and it should also be work which a man can do without
loss of self-respect. The difficulties in the way of providing inmates
with work related to their mental and physical capacities, come
both from industrialists and from the trade unions, who complain
that prison manufactures should not be allowed to go on the
market in competition with those produced by 'free labour' under
normal cost conditions. The goods produced have until now been
absorbed mainly by government departments, but their demands
for waste-paper baskets, hair mats and other typical prison pro-
ducts are insufficient to save the majority of men and women from
tasks which are given them primarily as a time-killing expedient.
Few prisoners (other than those in regional training prisons, who
undertake a definite course of training in one of a limited number
of skilled crafts) spend their working time doing things which
will in any way benefit them, mentally or physically, when they
are once more dependent upon their own labour for a living.

Connected with the problem of providing suitable work (which,
if it is really to help in restoring self-respect, must be saleable
work) is the more difficult and controversial problem of payment
to prisoners. No prisoner can 'earn' more than a few shillings
a week under present conditions. Few can buy enough tobacco
to satisfy them, let alone such aids to individual respect as
shaving-cream, hair-dressings and other simple toilet prepara-
tions, with the pittance they are now credited with weekly at
the canteens. Indeed, it is arguable that the present system of

prisoners' 'earnings' produces more problems for the administration than it solves. The average amount credited to a prisoner is rather more than three shillings per week: less than many of them are accustomed to giving a schoolboy son as pocket money when 'outside'. Such a miserable sum as this does nothing to increase a man's self-respect. By enabling him to buy half an ounce of tobacco a week legally, it merely helps the traffickers in tobacco (the 'barons') to establish and keep a hold on him.

If prisoners were paid the 'rate for the job' enjoyed by workers outside (and this would only be possible if they were able to do work of economic value) they might help to pay for their keep in prison, make some contribution to dependants outside (many of whom now receive help from the National Assistance Board), save a proportion of their wages to assist them on their release, and still have a larger sum for spending in prison than any enjoy at the moment.[1] But it is here that a moral question must be considered. If a man goes to prison as a result of a criminal act, and there enjoys full employment with pay, should not the first claim on his earnings be repayment to his victims of goods he has stolen, or compensation to them for any other damage he has inflicted upon them? If so, should the man himself be a charge on the state, and should his family be another charge on the state (by means of the National Assistance Board) while his earnings are thus distributed?

One of the strongest arguments in favour of providing work of an economic kind in prisons, and paying inmates a competitive wage, is that in this way prisoners would be subjected to the same incentives as we all are outside.

It is not easy under any circumstances for a man who has spent years shut away from the normal world to adjust himself when at last he is released. As far as possible, therefore, but only if it is therapeutically desirable, he should be subjected to competitive forces while in prison: to situations requiring perseverance, to problems requiring his personal decision. It is futile to send prisoners back into the normal world unless situations have been contrived in some way in the prisons to give them a chance of meeting successfully the sort of opposition and frustration which occurs in the life of every ordinary man and

[1] But the cost of institutional care (£356 per head in 1958, excluding new buildings, etc.) is such that it alone could swallow some men's entire wage.

woman in society. In several prisons 'pre-release courses' have been run, which strive to make men who are about to be discharged at least *aware*, once more, of the complications an unsheltered life imposes.[1] But it is insufficient to pose these problems intellectually. True preparation for release would ensure that such situations have been met and coped with inside the institution, and that the prisoner was made aware also of his individual psychological difficulties in trying to cope with them. The whole machinery of release should be in the charge of highly trained social therapists.

Some attempt has recently been made at Horfield Prison, Bristol, to familiarize long-term prisoners with the working world in the last few months of their sentences. There a hostel has been set up from which men with only six months of their time remaining can go out each day, as much as possible like free men, working in the city and drawing ordinary wages. They pay for their board and lodgings at the hostel, contribute towards their families' upkeep, and make compulsory savings towards their release. Eight hostels of this character have now been established at different institutions.

THE PRISONERS

Wherever men are held captive, a strong social network with distinct lines of dominance and subordination, its own code of behaviour and its own ties of loyalty, grows up among them, quite distinct and apart from any organizational structure which prison authorities may attempt to impose from above. The true life of a prison – a criminal prison or one for prisoners-of-war – exists almost independently of official rules and decisions; all but the vaguest indications of its character are hidden from the governor and his staff. Even the most skilful and sympathetic of prison officials is far out on the edge of this society and unable to make any permanent impact upon it.

Loyalty to an individual member of staff, loyalty strong enough to make an inmate break the behavioural code which has transmitted itself constantly through the changing population of the prison, is exceedingly rare. A prisoner is a man whom society has

[1] For an account of one such course (now discontinued) see Howard, D. L., 'Education as Social Rehabilitation' (*Adult Education Quarterly*, 1958).

marked with disapproval. Temporarily he is deprived of personal property and shut away from all those people whose affection or admiration gave him self-esteem and emotional security.[1] Most men experience acute shame when they are first given a prison sentence. Unless already of marked emotional instability, they suddenly become, at the moment of actual conviction, when suppressed fears of social ostracism and loss of status in the wide society come to the surface, more in need of some sign of approval, from any source, than at any time later in their prison careers. At this stage they are, perhaps, most susceptible to the approaches of a social worker. But we take too little advantage of this moment of sensitivity. The process of 'reception' in an English prison is still a degrading experience, serving only to exaggerate the feeling of isolation from society as a whole.[2] Inevitably, the prisoner seeks some comfort from the men all round him who are sharing the experience. The pains of emotional deprivation and social rejection are eased by joining in banter about the 'screws',[3] and he picks up the language of resentment, expressing personal inadequacy in hatred of all custodial staff, which is the currency of the inmate sub-culture. The prisoner's emotional condition at this stage is such that he *must* win social acceptance by the others. If he responds appreciatively to any sign of kindness on the part of an officer, he risks rejection again.

Thus all prisoners must conform to the inmates' social pattern and accept its values. Just as in a bad secondary modern school in a 'tough' area new boys must outwardly adopt the attitude and behaviour of the hooligan group instead of the manners teachers try to instil, so in a prison the new-comer must likewise show rejection of the custodial staff in order to enjoy some social ease with his equals. But in a prison outward acceptance is rarely sufficient. There are no holidays, or lengthy unsupervised visits by parents and friends during which the values of the wider society can be re-imposed. Imprisonment places men in a total environment constantly expressing hostility. The danger of prisoners communicating the methodology of crime to each other

[1] The men who form the recidivist core may never have had such emotional security. For them, the problem is how to help them to get it at all, not how to restore it to them.
[2] Prison Commissioners are aware of this problem. Some recent experiments in reception procedure are described in Chapter XVII.
[3] Prison Officers.

is one of which we are constantly aware, and one which prison rules attempt to prevent. But the greater danger is that by virtually forcing a convicted man into membership of a powerful social organism whose accepted ways of behaviour and whose framework of obligation and esteem are entirely directed against the conventions of the community outside prison, we are giving him education of the fullest and most effective kind in opposition to authority.

Unless the social structure of imprisonment can be fully analysed and understood[1] it will be difficult for any training which we attempt to impose from outside ever to be effective. Conformity to the *mores* of the inmate group is necessary to the offender, and far more influential than any 'straight talk' from the governor, or diagnostic interview with the psychiatrist. These occasions are opportunities for the prisoner to express the resentment he has so quickly absorbed: for expressing it at the interview itself, in misunderstanding or deliberate falsehood, or afterwards when the conversation is related to his mates in a way which gives additional support to established inmate attitudes.

It may be doubted if any research, unless carried out by a psychologist of very wide experience who can yet pass himself off among prisoners for a long time as one of themselves, can really reveal to us the power and complexity of the inmate social structure, or the ways in which conformity to it is constantly exacted. Frank Norman's book, *Bang to Rights*,[2] one of the few volumes of ex-prisoners' memoirs which have any sociological value, contains some glimpses of this subterranean system. He describes an interview in prison:

> Seeing all these people is the bigest wast of time you know, they all ask the same bleeding questions. So the best thing to do is give them all a different set of answers that way they get so confewsed that they don't know what's going on.
> So I get called up by this geezer.
> 'Well Norman you'll be go out in a few months now wont you?'
> What's the matter with this geezer, that's about the silleyest questions I ever been asked.

[1] Research toward this aim is now in progress at Pentonville Prison, with the full acknowledgement and encouragement of the Prison Commissioners.
[2] Secker & Warburg (London, 1958).

'Yes sir.'

'Do you think you'll go straight when you get out?'

'I don't know yet sir.'

'Now listen to me, this is probably the last chance you'll ever have.'

'This a chance sir?'

'Yes it is and it will be your last.'

'O.'

'Is there anything that you would like to talk to me about?'

'No sir.'

'Now look here I'm here to help you if I can.'

I made no reply to this. Why do all these people think that you need help all the time. The time I needed help was when I got captured almost two year's ago. Not now that it's all over.

'Alright that's all.'

I got up and walked out.

Despite his charmingly original spelling and punctuation, untouched by his publishers, Mr Norman's account of this incident must, I think, have been edited a little for public consumption. But add a few obscenities and a little more self-righteousness, and here we have the description of an interview with Assistant Governor/Medical Officer/Tutor Organizer/Psychologist or other senior prison official as I have heard it related by one inmate to another countless times. Very rarely is the barrier of opposition broken down; if it is, the prisoner omits the interviewer's discovery of a chink in his armour from the account he gives. Mr Norman has been 'inside' many times, and in many prisons, and his book effortlessly, even in its use of words, conveys the values of inmate society. Notice, for example, that he speaks of being 'captured', a word which we use instinctively instead of 'caught' when we imply that an enemy has got hold of us. The middle-class driver who breaks a speed limit when in a hurry is warned by his wife that he may get caught by the police. She never uses the word captured in this connexion, since her whole environment is one which recognizes the police as a body rightfully preserving order.

In another part of his book Mr Norman is sounding out the consolidated view of the prisoner society on the subject of war, and he is mildly surprised by it.

... But one interesting point was rased and that was what we would do if we were invaded, would we take the side of the enemy and kill all the screws and governors. Or would we forget that the screws were our enemys and fight on their side. I was quite surprised to hear that most of the geezers would fight with the screws against who ever it was that done the invadeing. Anyway as you know there was'nt any war to speak of so the situation did'nt arise. But it would have been a right gigle if it had, becase it is really surpriseing how much the screws are hated by the chaps.

War is something happening outside, to the society which has rejected them, but it is one of the few things, apparently, which can re-identify the inmate group with that society.

It would be stupid to suppose that all the attitudes and modes of behaviour adopted by a conformer in prison remain with him as mainsprings of thinking and acting after he leaves. Clearly they do not. But what is important to us in devising an effective form of treatment for the criminal, is that the majority of criminals are undoubtedly affected so completely by popular opinion when 'inside', and subordinate themselves so much to its pressures, that at the time when training can be attempted they are least able to accept it. It will never be accepted so long as the prisoner has no source of continuous social approval but his fellow-inmates, and so long as that source favours only behaviour which derides and belittles the custodial staff.

A dramatic development has taken place in our prisons within the last year in the use of group therapy. This is being carried out by ordinary prison officers with only a modicum of training, and it is clearly not yet at a stage where it can attempt direct rehabilitation (among other reasons, the officers are insufficiently trained in group dynamics for really deep therapy), but it is breaking down the opposition of prisoners to staff most effectively, and turning the pressure of prisoner opinion very much more toward the aims of the administration. The method has caught the imagination of the uniformed staff, from whom demands to extend it have come, and although some academic social scientists may doubt the wisdom of allowing any form of group therapy to be practised except by highly trained workers, it nevertheless appears that the climate of opinion in those institutions where it is being used already gives far more opportunities for conventional rehabilitative work than ever before. Group therapy now seems the most valuable weapon which can be used to break into the powerful prisoner-culture.[1]

THE METHOD OF ADMINISTRATION

A full analysis of the way in which our prisons are administered would be out of place here. Its chief defect is over-centralization.

I have heard it said that the governor of a prison is like the commander of a ship at sea, cut off from the world around him, and bound to make many important decisions on his own initiative, with recourse to the Admiralty only in occasional and exceptional circumstances. This delightful image is far from true. The freedom of a prison governor to act independently is very narrowly confined. He must observe a detailed and lengthy set of *Statutory Rules* so designed that methods of dealing with nearly all contingencies are ready prescribed for him to apply. He is encumbered by a litter of 'Minutes from Head Office' which arrive on his desk daily. Governors are required to get official permission before they make a common-sense decision on many points which are really only of local concern. Even before a tutor organizer can substitute a class in one subject for another, taking place at the same time, under the same teacher and at the same cost, a formal minute asking permission to do so must be sent

[1] Where an inmate's family can assist in his rehabilitation, its co-operation should be encouraged by every possible means. The attitudes of his closest friends are a major factor in the success of a prisoner in establishing normal behaviour after release. In this connexion, see in particular Fenton, Norman, *The Prisoner's Family* (California: Pacific Books, 1959), an account of the family counselling project carried out in the Californian prison system. The project was the first serious attempt to bring guidance procedure familiar in other fields of social work into play between prisoners and their families, with repeated contacts between prison staff and the immediate relatives of inmates from reception until release and during the period of parole. Its purpose was to inform wives and parents about the treatment given in the prisons and enlist their support for it, to show them how they could assist the inmate during and after his sentence, and to give them insight into his emotional needs. Therapeutic methods were employed to reveal to some relatives their own causal relationships to the offenders' troubles. Certain families received continuous attention from official or voluntary case-work agencies throughout the whole period of imprisonment. All were kept regularly informed of their own prisoner's progress in the institutions and given special guidance on his release.

to the Commissioners. No action can take place while a decision is awaited, but it is normally weeks and sometimes can be several months before a reply (or even a request for further information on the point) is received, by which time the original reason for the request may be almost forgotten.

The frequency with which governors have to refer to Horseferry House (the headquarters of the Prison Commission in London) must be a burden to the central administration as well as to the governors themselves. The situation has all the familiar failings of a large but clumsily organized administrative machine. It not only causes frustration even among senior members of the Prison Service; it stultifies enterprise and keeps a man who should be primarily an adviser, the leader of a team of social workers, tied to his office and far too remote from the daily problems of staff and prisoners. Governors, as a result, are apt to 'play safe', to work quietly along secure, traditional lines and put away ideas for improving the effectiveness of their institutions, rather than suffer the tedious process of describing, in minute after minute, the purpose of a proposed innovation, its significance in the local situation and its value in training, often only to receive an unexplained refusal at the end. The present system must also occupy Prison Commissioners unnecessarily in dealing with things which should really be the concern of trusted subordinates. Administrators of such responsibility and influence should have time in which to consider and evaluate ideas thrown up by young people lower in the ranks of their service. This time is now too often eaten away by much less-important and less-creative routine matters. Some further discussion of these problems is given in Chapter XVII.

THE PROBLEM OF STAFF

The English Prison and Borstal Service is a strongly disciplined hierarchical structure, more like one of the armed services than any normal social work department. Its staff is rigidly divided into 'subordinate' uniformed grades, which can be likened to non-commissioned ranks in the army, and 'superior' grades (the governors, assistant governors and professional workers). The Commissioners and Assistant Commissioners of Prisons, who direct the Service from Horseferry House, are usually men promoted from the governor ranks.

Within the subordinate grades of the Service there are but three ranks: Prison Officer, Principal Officer and Chief Officer. There are now three separate schemes by which carefully selected members of the uniformed staff can be promoted into the governor grades, after a special course of training at Wakefield, where the Service has its own training schools. But few officers are successful in this. The normal method of entry for governors is the 'direct method' by interview in response to advertisement in the national Press. With such a narrow prospect of advancement, promotion in the officer grade is painfully slow. Once he has passed out of the probationary period and his appointment to the Service is confirmed, an officer can usually expect to wait twelve years at least before there is a likelihood of achieving Principal Officer rank.

It is the ordinary prison officer who, in present circumstances, has a closer and more constant contact with individual prisoners than any other official. He is present at all stages of the inmates' day; he supervises them at work and in recreation, he unlocks them and locks them up again, he marches them from place to place, he even sits alongside them in chapel. Few people who have worked in an English prison can fail to have been impressed by the enlightened interest – in some cases almost devotion – displayed by many prison officers in their extremely monotonous duties. The job carries with it free accommodation, a uniform allowance, and a wage which is a little above the national average for skilled workers. But the officer is a member of an organization in which discipline is strict and formal, one in which the prospect of rising to the highest rank is remote, and one which requires him daily to work with men full of resentment against him and never slow to show it.

The main difficulty faced by the ordinary prison officer today is that he can never be quite sure what his duties are, and how he is to carry them out. Before his appointment is made permanent he is given a brief course of instruction at the Wakefield training school. Although the greater part of this course is occupied with the traditional procedures for maintaining discipline and security given in the framework of a 'fortress prison', trainees are introduced to some modern ideas in the treatment of prisoners, and are encouraged to take a sympathetic interest in their difficulties. Too often they find, on returning to the establishment in which they are to work, that the senior uniformed officers pay only lip service to all but the disciplinary aspects of the job, or openly sneer at the idea of taking a positive role in treatment. And yet the governor and his assistants, who may well wish to encourage the best concepts implanted at Wakefield, are usually remote figures, to be saluted on sight, for whom frank, open discussion of prison problems with officers is a rare occurrence.[1] The staff who immediately supervise a young prison officer – the Principal Officers next above him in rank – are too often men who grew old in the traditional ways of the Service before 'all that soft stuff they put over at Wakefield nowadays' made any impression at all on training methods. And yet the enthusiastic young officer with ideas of social service (he is not as rare as some writers on prison matters and some prison governors would have us believe) is a man who badly needs encouragement and guidance. He has a position of immense responsibility in which he can, given skilled advice, have an immeasurably good influence upon individual prisoners. It is he, fresh from the world outside prison and as yet unspoiled by the hardened formality of approach so many of his seniors have adopted, who is most likely to draw inmates away from their private world of corruption and compromise.

It is almost as difficult for a junior prison officer to work against the climate of opinion on the staff he has joined, as it is for the inmate to stand out as an individual against the embraces of the subculture I have described earlier. Unlike the governor, he is not only the focus of resentment from below; he is also dependent upon approval from officers ranked above him in the same institution. Moreover, he usually lives in or near the prison, in official quarters, with other prison officers, their wives and their families as his most frequent social contacts when not on duty. If he appears to be less severe toward prisoners and to take a more sympathetic interest in them than the majority of his colleagues, social difficulties in private life may be added to the unpopularity he has experienced at work.

[1] The recently introduced Staff Consultative Committees have by no means solved this problem. They are held but once a quarter, officers are merely represented on them, and so great a consciousness of rank is displayed that relaxed, open discussion of treatment problems is virtually impossible. Nevertheless the principle of introducing these committees is excellent: it is part of an attack on the human relations problems of prison administration which the Prison Commissioners show signs of forcing on with in many ways.

One of the most encouraging innovations recently introduced by the Prison Commissioners (who are not entirely unaware of the difficulties in which their staff have to work) is the so-called Norwich System. At Norwich, a small local prison in the charge of a governor who has himself been promoted from the ranks, individual officers have each been made responsible for a small group of prisoners. They have been asked to study the records of these men closely, and to adopt an advisory role, giving their groups the sort of attention which a probation officer might be expected to give to his charges. The effect of this experiment upon the officers' morale, and upon the whole atmosphere of the prison, has been quite remarkable. For the first time, the staff have clearly, without any doubt at all, been given a positive function in treatment, and they have responded to it magnificently. Prisoners coming from Norwich on discharge or on transfer to another institution show more definite signs of loyalty to individual officers and to the régime as a whole, and are less completely absorbed by feelings of social rejection, more lively and hopeful in outlook, than ever they were before the introduction of the system. The officers have enjoyed more 'work satisfaction' and have a greater sense of the 'worthwhileness' of their duties than they would have had in a prison run on traditional lines.

The experiment at Norwich is continuing, and the Prison Commissioners have extended it to many other small local prisons and some of medium size. The chief difficulty in making it general in the local establishments is that of temporary overcrowding. Such a system must be weakened in an institution which becomes suddenly flooded with new arrivals at short notice, so that the ratio of staff to prisoners is repeatedly upset. Although by no means a complete answer to the problem of winning over inmates to the side of authority – indeed, group counselling gives much more striking opportunities for this – the Norwich System has gone part of the way toward that object and it is enormously encouraging that so much has been achieved by it without intensive special training of the staff concerned.

The 'superior' grades of prison staffs are not without problems. Although their chances of rising in the Service are a little better than those of uniformed officers, promotion is still slower for them than in most organizations comparable with it. The difficulty which most frequently presents itself immediately to the new arrival in these grades is that of dealing with the resentment shown against him by so many of the uniformed officers. It is inevitable, perhaps, that men who know their chances of reaching the highest ranks in their chosen field of work should feel antagonistic toward those who are placed in authority over them (a more definite authority than that which applies in business concerns) without any previous experience in the peculiar affairs of prison administration. The best of the older prison officers adopt towards the young assistant governor an attitude rather like that of a good Sergeant Major in the army toward a newly commissioned subaltern, but a young 'A.G.' is fortunate if he can entirely avoid the sort of criticism youthful subalterns often receive from the less tolerant N.C.O.s in the army. There are indications that the Prison Commissioners are at last paying attention to the need for recruiting assistant governors with some qualification in social science. Very few of the governors now in the Prison Service have had any form of professional or academic training in social work. A one-year course of training (including rudimentary instruction in social case-work techniques) is now given to all new direct entrants at the Wakefield training school, in conjunction with Leeds University, but this, of course, is not nearly enough. If prisons are to be genuinely therapeutic communities their senior officials, at least, must not only be trained in all the relevant branches of sociology and psychology; they might with advantage also have had considerable experience in normal social work in a civilian setting. The prison governor is a man who deals with people who are often severely damaged as social beings. He not only needs the intellectual equipment provided by a sociological and psychological training to help him in the task of rehabilitating them; he needs, before he is placed in a position of such authority, to have the tact and judgement in dealing with morally weak and emotionally disturbed people which only years of experience in social work under trained supervision can bring. It cannot be denied that much excellent work is now being done in the Prison Service by officials without this training and experience. But prisons are not the places in which they should have had to learn from their mistakes.

The 'superior staff' of the Prison Service are hindered in their work primarily by an administrative flaw. All governors and assistant governors are subject to removal from one prison to another at the will of the Establishment Branch of the Prison Commission.[1] It is rare for them to stay in one institution for more than three years, and since the senior officials in each prison are transferred at different times, it is impossible for a really effective team of governors to be built up in any one of them. Prisons vary enormously in the administrative problems they present. They vary in size from institutions holding little more than a hundred prisoners, to vast establishments with a population of over a thousand. In character they vary from a completely 'open' prison like Leyhill, where the inmates enjoy a considerable degree of physical freedom and can also organize for themselves many of the institution's activities, to a maximum security prison such as Nottingham, where discipline is at its most rigid. When a governor is transferred he must spend several months in the new establishment before he has its problems sufficiently in his grasp to make any significant impact upon them: before he can know his new assistant governors, the new chaplain, tutor organizer, welfare officer, and other senior officials well enough to handle them sympathetically and well: before he can really make the best of the human and physical factors available there for the work of rehabilitation. It may be less than a year after he has grown sufficiently familiar with those problems and people to administer them really well, when he is given yet another post, in a place where there is an entirely different situation to be faced. The governor who rules 'strictly by the book' is, of course, uninfluenced by the unique set of personalities each institution represents; he does not even attempt to interlock them. But surely the Prison Commissioners themselves do not regard a governor so stilted in his approach as this as the ideal? It is not unknown for assistant governors to be transferred from a large maximum security prison to work in an open Borstal institution, where an entirely different personality is desirable. The disadvantages to the development of sound and continuous policies presented by this apparently quixotic practice of switching senior officials from one place to another are obvious. It also presents serious

[1] The activities of the Establishment Branch are not, however, entirely capricious. Transfers are made to fill vacancies caused by promotions or the opening of new establishments. In a service which is expanding rapidly, frequent changes are very difficult to avoid, although their effects may be undesirable.

personal difficulties to the men concerned, and to their wives and families. Children must be uprooted from school every few years (few prison officials can afford to educate them entirely outside the state system) and as the whole family wanders periodically from one part of the country to another, from country village to industrial city, from Yorkshire to Devon, from Sussex to Lancashire, contact is lost with many friends. There is no group of people more in need of a stable social life to support them in their intensely demanding and difficult work than prison governors, but the transfer system is such that normal social contacts can be built up only with extreme difficulty.

The problems discussed in this chapter are by no means the only difficulties facing our prison system, nor has full expression been given even to them. But if those selected here for discussion could alone be solved we might, perhaps, be well on the way to turning our prisons into the therapeutic communities they should be. A writer who merely states problems is performing a very limited and quite uncreative service; to propose solutions to those problems is far more difficult. As has been said earlier, the form of the future prisons, their design, the way they are staffed and administered, and the sort of training which is to be given in them, must await the time when research has increased our knowledge of the criminal and shown us more clearly how he can be reformed.

In the years of waiting we cannot stand still. Something must be done to make the work of individual rehabilitation more effective at once, and the present Home Secretary and the Prison Commissioners now in office, who have shown themselves most responsive to new ideas and eager to test them practically, seem determined to take action.

L

CHAPTER XVII

INTO THE FUTURE

A complete rebuilding of all the prisons of England as security institutions is politically impossible. It would involve spending at least one hundred million pounds: a sum which no government is likely to sanction in the near future. Even if our huge annual expenditure on armaments were drastically cut it would be grossly optimistic to hope that capital on this scale would become available to the Prison Service. There are many other social services well ahead of prisons in the queue for money, and all of them have a greater immediate appeal to the taxpayer and therefore a greater political importance. Most of our hospitals are quite as out of date as our prisons, and in some parts of the country they have similar problems of overcrowding. Far too many of our children are still being educated in schools erected before 1870, where it is impossible for their teachers to use really modern methods. The health services and the educational system are used by the majority of the population, who are influenced directly, at first hand, by their efficiency. But even at a crisis of delinquency such as we are now experiencing, the nation expects to get its penal services on the cheap. This is primarily because most of the electorate has no clear idea of how effective properly designed services of this kind could prove. When the problem of crime is discussed in the 'local' or over the tea-cups, argument usually centres on the efficiency of the police, whose work with criminals is more immediately apparent than that of the Prison Service. But no matter how successful the police may become in catching thieves in the act of stealing, or in detecting their plans beforehand, they can make no impact on the genesis of delinquency. The police deal with the results of a social system which throws up criminals; true crime prevention is concerned with analysing that system and altering those aspects of it which make some of us contravene the law.

The most important work of crime prevention is the seeking

out of delinquency-prone children and youths, and so arranging the social pressures at work upon them that they have alternative outlets for expression. When the production of cheap cotton in the early nineteenth century first made it possible for most of the population to wear easily washable underclothes, an important cause of contagious epidemics was removed; when, during the war, supplies of sugar were restricted, tooth decay among young children was arrested. Most of our efforts towards the abatement of crime must be of this character: we want to find the equivalent in social medicine of cheap cotton pants. We want to stop concentrating on the brushing of teeth which are already starting to decay, and turn our attention also to the original cause of decay.

It must be recognized that among the urban wage-earners who form the majority of the criminal population, the strength of the family as a social unit has been severely weakened with every increase in their economic prestige.[1] The social ends to which the greater part of our population devotes its increases in purchasing power, are ends which often directly oppose the authoritarian structure typical of the working-class family fifty years ago. In this stratum of society a child becomes independent of his parents' moral attitudes even while still at school: hence the difficulties faced by many schoolmasters in the industrial cities. For the majority of urban children, approval by the family, with its tight and very strongly expressed system of values, is discarded in favour of the more superficial and more immediately appealing judgements of teen-age friends at 14 or even earlier. The unmarried teen-agers form a strong spending group whose special demands are well met by commercial enterprise. Their colourful clothes, their comic magazines, their musical preferences, their coffee-bars, all reflect the emotional insecurity and restlessness which is characteristic of this stage in psychological development: a stage through which young people fifty years ago were carefully directed by parents whose value judgements still carried great authority. The process should not be described dramatically as a revolt against parental domination, nor should it be said that that maligned abstraction, the modern parent, has abdicated his

---

[1] Hoggart, R., *The Uses of Literacy* (Chatto & Windus, 1957), is an effective discussion of the ways in which an increase in its income affects the pattern of working-class family behaviour.

responsibilities. The whole development has taken place inconspicuously alongside the rise of the 'working class' to economic prosperity. This rise, with its concomitant alteration in the purchasing power held by different members of each family, has brought about a change in the structure of family authority. School-leavers of 15 now frequently have more money to spend on non-essentials (non-essentials enjoyed very largely outside the family group and in contrast to the leisure habits of parents) than their fathers. The development is also related to the lowering of the age at which children acquire some degree of physical maturity. To slang curiously dressed youths by calling them 'Teddy-boys' (a phrase which always has overtones of social disapproval) is to be at the least unhelpful to them, and at most provocative of further displays of the independence they are still not quite certain whether they have in fact achieved.

The cotton pants of the delinquency problem may be provided when we recognize that adolescents are now in need of some definitely acceptable authoritarian structure outside their homes, of which they can become voluntary members, and whose judgements they are therefore likely to accept. This is not an attack on the family. The power to exact conformity to every part of the behaviour pattern approved in the wide society is lost to most working-class families already, as far as adolescents are concerned. This is a plea that we should accept the urgent need to provide some alternative way of performing a social function once performed automatically in working-class homes, but which is now the responsibility of no alternative agency. Indeed, parental status in this, the largest stratum of society, would be strengthened if parents could give support to a set of values being applied to their children outside the home. To be effective, these values must be applied by some organizational device attractive and acceptable to 'teen-agers'. An experiment of the kind here suggested is being carried out in a small way in Brighton, a town which, in the profusion of superficial entertainments it provides, and with a large transient population conspicuously spending money on pleasurable activities, has a serious problem of juvenile delinquency. A most enlightened committee of enquiry into the needs of youth in Brighton has recommended that the local education authority should set up a coffee-house of its own, equipped with all the gaudy delights of most immediate appeal

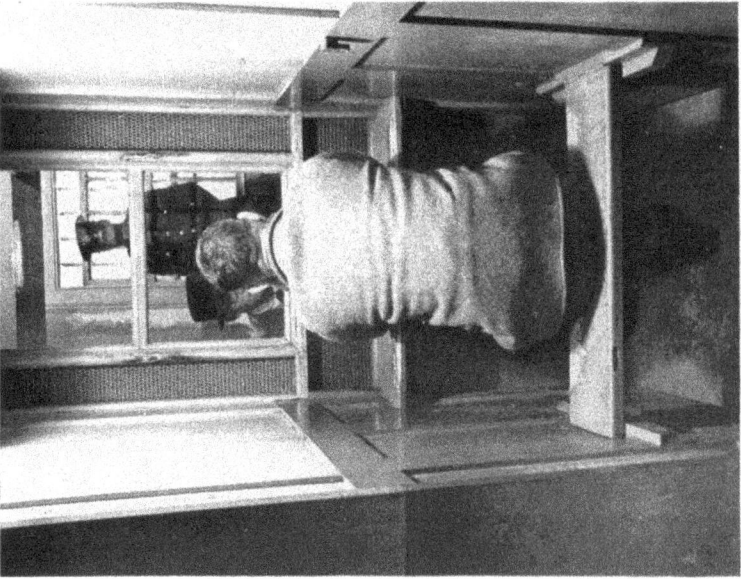

Holloway Prison. Interior of a cell

A prison visit, Wandsworth

to young wage-earners, but with properly trained youth workers in charge of it. This attempt is nearer the heart of the real problem of adolescent criminality than the estimable experiment with youth liaison officers run by the Liverpool police. Crime prevention of this character is less tangibly effective than herding brightly dressed boys and girls into police vans after a fight at a dance-hall, and in the present state of public opinion and knowledge it will be given far less support. But it is far more likely to succeed in killing delinquency at the stage where it grows most healthily.

Just as all the improvements in personal hygiene which took place a hundred years ago have left us with a diminished problem of physical disease, a truly revolutionary approach to treating the actual causes of delinquency before they affect the individual will leave us with some problem of crime, although a smaller one. However satisfactory a policy of keeping people out of prisons may become, there will still be a need for prisons.

PRISON BUILDINGS

Even if it were politically possible to start a complete rebuilding of our prisons, I do not think it would be desirable. The best methods which could be applied today may well be superseded in the future by others, needing different facilities and accommodation of different design. We do not want, at vast expense, to erect buildings which are destined to be as great a handicap to our successors as the early Victorian prisons are to us now. Furthermore, the numbers to be accommodated in prisons will not remain static. They may dwindle quite rapidly if effective preventive measures are applied to check the growth of crime. They may, as a result of economic and social changes as yet unforeseen, rise yet higher than they are now. But one thing is clear: we want no more large prisons. All penal institutions, of whatever type, should be so small that face-to-face relationships are possible among all members of staff and all inmates together. A genuinely therapeutic community must be a small community, in which policy decisions are personally conveyed, not transmitted from a distant, rarely seen group of senior officials distinctly separate from the main body of staff and from the inmates. The need for economy in prison building is no hindrance to the establishment in the near future of institutions for fifty or sixty prisoners in large country houses. One of the few advantages of our present prisons is that they occupy land of considerable value. There would be little difficulty in disposing of the sites on which most of them stand if local authorities did not object to the erection of private factory or office buildings in their place.

The total evacuation of existing prisons at a stroke of the pen is not envisaged here. Overcrowding is now so serious that over six thousand men are confined three in a cell; the first of the newly acquired small prisons should be used to relieve pressure in the present buildings, and then, as more new properties are obtained, the most unsatisfactory of the security prisons, such as Armley Prison, Leeds,[1] and Pentonville Prison, London, can be discarded. The funds available for prisons are such that by no means all the old walled buildings, and perhaps not even a majority, could be abandoned within twenty years. For those which remain, the plan (advocated by the Howard League for Penal Reform) of erecting walls to seal off the larger cell blocks from one another and running them as separate community-prisons is an expedient which would at least create institutions small enough to be run on a personal basis, with few enough inmates to make a personal relationship with all the staff really possible. Such establishments would still lack the educational, social and training facilities a modern prison needs; they would still be abnormal, fortress-like buildings expressing isolation from the community in every stone; but they would be a great improvement on the urban prisons as they now stand, and with a good staff equipped with genuinely rehabilitative techniques, they could be far more successful. At a smaller cost than the six hundred thousand pounds spent on Everthorpe Hall, we could in this way acquire a whole series of reasonably effective security institutions.

The danger which lies in all compromise schemes is that they may be accepted so enthusiastically, as offering considerable economies, that completely new building work will be reduced to an absolute minimum. But so energetic and far seeing has been Mr R. A. Butler in his tenure of the Home Office, that already the

[1] Erected in 1847 to accommodate 350 men, but with a population in 1959 of nearly one thousand. Even if expansion of the buildings on the existing site has been thought desirable, the clutter of industrial shops round it makes it quite impossible.

Prison Commissioners are committed to an expenditure of forty million pounds on new buildings. It should always be kept in mind by the most enthusiastic and idealistic of prison reformers that some proportion of the men sent to prison must, in their own interest as well as that of the general population, be held in security. The adapted buildings proposed here would remain secure, but even after alteration they would be most unsuitable for the permanent detention of men and women in maximum security for long sentences. The greater part of the funds now forthcoming is being used for new institutions for men of this character. An impressive architectural opportunity has been presented to the Prison Commissioners: an opportunity to design an English prison which will really express up-to-date penal methods.

There is now an entirely new buildings research group at Horseferry House, which, after visiting Scandinavian and other countries to learn from their experience, is considering a completely new approach to the problem of prison construction. We can expect a complete break away from traditional principles in this field, although Hindley Prison, near Wigan, now in course of building, was planned and begun before the research group was formed ('The Commissioners concede that, designed four or five years ago as it was, [Everthorpe] is already a little out of date.' [1]) Hindley Prison is modified from the Everthorpe plan in that its cells will be in solid corridors instead of all facing into a central hall. This form of cell arrangement has already been virtually discarded by the American Federal Bureau of Prisons. The *Handbook of Correctional Institution Design and Construction*, published by the Federal Bureau of Prisons in 1949, well before the first brick was laid at Hindley, gives it as the considered opinion of the senior American penal authority that

> In regard to cells, the fundamental item in institutional housing facilities, the Federal Bureau has shown the waste and futility involved in providing only maximum-security cells inside any institution, save, perhaps, for *super-security* prisons. The penitentiary of the future is bound to be one of mixed-custody construction, equipped with some ultra-secure inside cells, some less, but adequately secure outside cells *and a number of medium security outside rooms.*[2]

[1] *The Times*, 29 May 1959.   [2] The italics are mine.

The Federal Bureau of Prisons is by no means a revolutionary body. Moreover, the American conception of a super-security prison envisages the holding of prisoners far more violent and of far greater potential danger to the public than almost any we have to deal with in England. None of the prisons in this country even approaches the super-security establishments of the Federal Bureau in the restrictions applied to movement of prisoners and the precautions taken against escape.

A few security cells are needed, of course, in any prison, for long-term offenders. But a far better (and a far cheaper) way of housing prisoners is the cubicle method in open dormitories. Construction of such dormitories is a little more expensive than the building of open dormitories of the military type, but it is the most inexpensive type of accommodation which offers some element of privacy. It has the additional advantage of giving light, air and space to each inmate such as he could only have otherwise in a large room of his own. Furthermore, washing and lavatory facilities with running water can be provided for all the men in the room, and they can have free access to toilets even when the dormitory itself is locked or closely supervised. The sanitation in our existing prisons is a national disgrace. Men are locked in for more than twelve hours out of every twenty-four in some of them, without access to a lavatory. It must be remembered that three men are commonly locked up together in a cell under these conditions, and that when the existing programme of prison building, outlined in the recent White Paper,[1] and its more hazy 'future' building proposals are completed, there will still be 1,500 men subjected to this utterly degrading and unhygienic daily experience.[2]

THE PROVISION OF WORK

The Prison Commissioners have made some impact on the problem of providing suitable work in prisons by appointing a man of wide industrial experience to advise upon it. The White Paper

[1] *Penal Practice in a Changing Society.*
[2] The Prison Commission hopes that a new security prison at Blundeston, Suffolk, will be begun in 1960. This 'security training prison' is designed to hold 300 men in four cell blocks, each containing a dormitory for eight men as well as separate cells.

promises that greater attempts will be made in the future to achieve co-operation with the Trades Union Congress and the organizations representing employers in industry so that prison labour can be used on contract work for normal industry: a practice which is in general use in most western European countries. The basic issue in the introduction of this practice is that of deciding how far individual prisons should specialize in particular industries. Nearly all prison workshops now in use are too small to make production units of a scale competitive with outside contractors, and it is doubtful whether the cost of re-arranging in them sufficiently large and well-equipped space is justified if there is to be any hope of abandoning these institutions or converting them each into several 'self-supporting' smaller communities. Continental industrial practice should not be adopted, however desirable it is to have men working usefully and producing things of genuine economic value, if the more essential need for smaller prisons is then overlooked. Prisons must not become places where industrial production is the first or even the major priority. The sole aim of prisons is to rehabilitate men and women, and the point of revising inmates' working conditions is to help that aim, not to add yet another difficulty to the many which now hinder it.

The prison a man is sent to should never be chosen in the light solely of his previous industrial experience. That could be taken into consideration, but the first object is to send men to the prisons (and there should be a very wide variety indeed) where their individual social rehabilitation is most likely to be achieved. There may be many cases where men in need of attention of a particular kind are not the most suitable for the sort of production carried out in the institutions where that special form of treatment is available. In such circumstances, manufacturing in those institutions must suffer.

Concerning the payment of prisoners, it is obvious that an 'economic wage rate' cannot be given until output is comparable with that of outside industry. The questions raised immediately above make it unlikely that this production can be achieved in many fields. An international investigation into the question of making normal wages payable to prisoners is now being held under the auspices of the United Nations Organization.

Most of the work performed by prisoners will inevitably be

work requiring little training and, for the most part, no more than average intelligence. It is not inconceivable that if the prison of the future is a tiny institution, and the prison population is therefore more widely and evenly dispersed throughout the country than it is now, a large proportion of the men and women can be permitted to spend a part of their sentences, at least, working for local employers in farming and general labouring duties outside the prison buildings. Many open prisons already practise this idea on a small scale where there are no local trade-union hindrances. The escape risks involved in such a scheme have been shown to be minimal, and the objections sometimes raised by local trade-union branches might well be withdrawn if a joint sub-committee representing both the Trades Union Congress and the Prison Commissioners were set up to review common difficulties as they occur.

THE PRISONERS

The first requirement to be insisted upon in the future treatment of prisoners is adequate diagnosis. In all cases, the newly arrived prisoner's background, including his family situation, his work history, educational history and his previous brushes with the law, should be explored thoroughly by a trained social worker. If the social worker deems it necessary, this general procedure should be followed up by a more thorough individual medical examination than all prisoners are normally given, and by a special psychiatric investigation. Unless we know what social pressures have been at work upon the man, what emotional difficulties he has, and how far treatment has been attempted in the past, we cannot attempt to treat him adequately in prison.

In some prisons[1] new-comers have been given an 'induction period' of two or three weeks while classification has been considered, and during this time the staff have been able to show greater interest in them as individuals than is possible when (as is usual) fresh arrivals are thrown into the rough normal life of the prison almost at once, without preparation for it. This excellent practice is by no means general, and the White Paper regrets that it cannot be generally adopted in present conditions.

The major difficulty in training prisoners effectively is the

[1] Notably at Cardiff and at Lewes.

development among them of a culture quite separate and apart from the organizational structure imposed from above, and strongly hostile to the custodial staff. This we have seen. If a diagnostic 'induction period', during which new-comers were kept entirely away from the main body of prisoners and given close personal attention, were made general, and if the institutions to which they were sent afterwards could really be small face-to-face communities, with all the officers trained in distinctly therapeutic roles, the growth of such an opposing culture among them would be considerably weakened.

THE METHOD OF ADMINISTRATION

Decentralization of the powers now tightly held by the Prison Commissioners in London is essential if the prisons are to function really efficiently in the future. Area offices of the Commission might be set up throughout the country, from which administration could be carried out on a much more personal level than it is now. There should be at least one man of Assistant Commissioner (or possibly Comissioner) status near enough each group of prisons to visit them very frequently and to familiarize himself with the general outline of each in its particular task and in the problems its governor faces. Such a man could give decisions, when consulted, which were really relevant to the local situation which called for them. The function of the Prison Commissioners should be rather less like that of a military G.H.Q. and rather more like that of Her Majesty's Inspectorate of Education. They should not be remote creatures rarely seen by ordinary members of their staffs, whose visits are preceded by the sort of 'dressing up' a brass hat from the War Office takes for granted when he goes to a barracks. They should be in the capacity of advisors, as are the inspectors of education; they should be people who carry ideas from one place to another and offer solutions to individual problems in the light of their greater experience; people who *have* *time* to show genuine understanding.

Some members of the Prison Service imagine their Commissioners at work as harassed, over-pressed individuals continually fighting back against rising waves of paper communications, and periodically retreating further up the beach so that delay in answering minutes created by their own organization further increases. It is clear that they are grossly overworked, and, inevitably under the present organization, are far too much concerned with comparatively unimportant details. Whether centralization remains or not, there must be more people at Horseferry House to deal with day-to-day routine administration, leaving the senior officials of the Commission free to get to know the prisons and the staffs in their charge, free to absorb the spate of current criminological literature, nearly all of which should influence them to some degree, and free to plan. At the moment they cannot, surely, have sufficient peace in which to consolidate the results of current experiments and to initiate more with the care and foresight which are necessary.

There should be more men at the headquarters of the Prison Service who, by training and experience, are specialists in the many types of human activity carried out in prison and Borstal training: men who are able to evaluate professionally the work of psychologists, education officials, social workers, medical officers, welfare officers and all the other men and women of advanced training in different fields who must increasingly come on to their staffs in the future. If prisons are to become therapeutic communities, they will be staffed by senior officials (governors, assistant governors and professional men), a large part of whose time is devoted to the encouragement and supervision of officers who themselves have some degree of training in social science. The most up-to-date and advanced theories and methods of the behaviour sciences must therefore be at the finger-tips of some of the administrators at Horseferry House. It is useless for any organization to employ a highly trained specialist if the organization itself is not qualified to direct and evaluate his work; it is tragic for him and harmful to the organization if continual misunderstanding of his efforts forces him to leave.

THE STAFF

I once asked a group of prison officers if they would not prefer to work in civilian clothes, as Borstal officers do, instead of wearing a uniform. All were unanimously in favour of retaining their uniforms, and one even went so far as to suggest that governors should wear a uniform too, 'like a colonial governor does'. I do not think these officers were thinking primarily of the wear-and-

New Hall Camp, near Wakefield. The first 'Open Prison', 1934

tear saved to their ordinary clothing. The discussion which followed made it clear that to the average officer his uniform is a symbol of authority: it is the possession which most of all marks him off from the prisoners he is daily concerned with. If the officers in question had been properly trained to deal with difficult human beings (to deal with them, that is, other than by shouting at them and threatening to 'throw the book at them' if they do not obey) I think they would have considered uniforms a disadvantage in their work. Every man, even the most unthinking lance-corporal, becomes a little less a human being and rather more an impersonal mechanism when he dons a uniform giving him authority. For people whose work in the future must be primarily devoted to bridging a gap of resentment between themselves and men of particularly unstable social behaviour, a uniform is a distinct handicap. So, too, are all the other trappings of military discipline which live on in the Prison Service. It should be as ludicrous for a prison officer to salute his governor in the institutions of the future as it would be now for a psychiatric social worker to salute her psychiatrist before getting down to discussion of case histories with him. If all of this goes it will make for greater social ease among all grades of staff in the Prison Service. It will also raise the status of the prison officer in the eyes of the prisoners, the general public and the 'superior' staff of his own organization.

Prison officers need, in the future, to be given a training which makes the understanding of human behaviour difficulties the central focus of all their work. They cannot all be skilled caseworkers and it is not really desirable that they should be. But their training at Wakefield should make it clear that they are instruments of social treatment just as nurses in a hospital are the instruments of medical treatments prescribed and supervised by a physician. Some officers will have to spend much of their time doing routine tasks in the future, just as nearly all of them are now submitted to a working day of monotonous boredom. But they will, if taught their new tasks well, readily accept the duller custodial aspects of their work, just as the hospital nurse endures uninteresting hours when she feels she is not directly occupied in helping the sick. The educational standard of the average prison officer is not as low as many prison governors frequently imply when discussing their work. I am sure that most of them are quite capable of good work as agents of the new therapeutic régime: their response to new opportunities at Norwich, and the eagerness with which they have received the idea of group therapy are indications of this. And as soon as the work of a prison officer becomes the work of human interest that recruiting posters claim it to be, recruitment from young people of good academic education will be greatly stimulated.

If the Prison Commissioners were to adopt a definitely social-therapeutic policy, they should not introduce it stealthily, hoping the change would be so gradual that officers would slowly acclimatize themselves to it: such a period of change would increase the confusion and uncertainty prison officers already suffer, to a point at which it might well become unbearable. It should be introduced with a flourish, and it should be fully explained, in detail, so that the officer would know exactly what his position in the future was to be, and exactly how he was expected to work. Inevitably, after the sound of trumpets had died away, it would be a long time before buildings and staff necessary for the full implementation of the new approach became available; but the goal would already have been declared, and the Commissioners and their governors should at once adopt the attitude of encouragement and stimulation, constantly reminding officers of the completed form, while its shaping was taking place.

As reorganization proceeded, and people of higher academic achievement were attracted into the ranks of the Prison Service, it would become easier for governor and assistant governor posts to be filled from the officer grade. But the people considered for promotion should at the very least be of sufficient intellect to undertake a university diploma course in social science: unless they had outstanding personality traits, of value in the treatment of delinquents, this training would not be enough: they should be trained further, in generic case-work, in group dynamics and in management techniques. And having obtained the necessary academic background, all should spend at least two years in normal social work, on secondment from the Prison Service, before taking up their new posts. It is absolutely necessary for men who can have such enormous influence upon the lives of extremely unfortunate fellow-beings, and who are ultimately to direct their training, to feel at first hand the stresses these people are so often subjected to before they arrive in prison. They must, too, understand the inner workings of the social network which prisoners are to link up with again on their release. One may stagger at the cost of training senior prison officials in this way: it is so much cheaper to take totally untrained men, as we do now, and fling them into the prison situation after only a minimum of instruction about the working of the human mind. But if we want successful prisons, the work of a prison governor is going to be the most all-embracing and the most difficult social work a man can attempt to perform. It is work not only difficult in itself, and not only calling for wide academic knowledge and considerable insight (if it takes the form suggested here), but also intensely frustrating work. Men and women engaged upon it must be able to understand their own emotional attitudes and the pressures which influence themselves.

The method of appointing governors direct from outside the Prison Service should not be cast aside. But something more must be asked of candidates than a satisfactory general education and an interest in social work. Ideally, the field should be restricted entirely to good honours graduates in the social sciences, who have had experience in a field as relevant as probation, and who have taken that experience not merely to qualify for the Prison Service but to serve the people it cares for. But the demand for graduates in sociology is strong, and by restricting the field in this way it is doubtful whether sufficient candidates of the right personality in addition to university training of sufficient standard would be forthcoming. Nevertheless, some higher standard should be imposed than we now insist upon, and the fullest use should be made of the direct entry method to ensure a constant infusion of lively people, full of initiative and full of ideas which years of service in prisons have not made stale.

If one could take apart any social institution overnight and re-assemble it according to an ideal plan ready to work again the next morning, without wondering where money can be obtained, where staff of the right calibre can appear from, and with certainty that the plan itself was perfect, there would be an enormous saving in human resentment, frustration and worry. Any set of changes which are proposed, and certainly those which are carried out, in an organization which concerns thousands of people, is bound to hurt some, to unsettle others and to worry many. Few of us can

accept alterations in matters closely affecting us without re-
garding them as personal criticism, at least in implication. The
ideas put forward here for improving the Prison Service are not
intended to destroy, but to build upon good work which has
been done for many years by hundreds of devoted men and women
in the Prison Service, from individual Commissioners down to the
most modest of officers. I would be extremely sorry if I knew
that any individual in the Prison Service who has read this book
was hurt by anything said directly in it, or anything which its
comments and suggestions might seem to imply. Nor must the
suggestions made in Part Two of the book be taken as criticisms
of the Prison Commissioners as a body; I am well aware that their
thinking and their plans for future developments are far more
enlightened and much farther advanced than most critics are
aware of, or credit them with. The general reader must not assume
that none of the innovations proposed in this book would be
officially acceptable. The Prison Commissioners have a far more
difficult task than their critics: that of analysing new ideas and
determining whether they would really be workable. This is a
task that only they can do, and they are doing it most
imaginatively.

Appendices

THE NEW PRISON, LEWES

The ground plan of a small English prison of the Pentonville type. This building, completed in 1854, is now in use as a Young Prisoners' Institution (i.e. for boys under 21 years of age, sentenced to imprisonment rather than to Borstal training). Most of the prisons in English county towns are built on this pattern.

1 Cells
2 Officers
3 Trade Instructors' Room
4 Surgery
5 Corridor
6 Inspection Hall
7 Prisoners' Visiting-rooms
8 Magistrates' Room
9 Surgeon's Bedroom
10 Surgeon's Parlour
11 Waiting-room
12 Governor's Office
13 Governor's Clerk's Office
14 Solicitor's Room
15 Chief Warder's Bedroom
16 Chief Warder's Sitting-room
17 Infirmary Ward
18 Infirmary Warder
19 Debtors' Day Room
20 Matron's Bedroom
21 Matron's Parlour
22 Entrance
23 Day Room, 1st-Class Debtors
24 Day Room, 2nd-Class Debtors
25 Inclined Plane
26 Infirmary Airing Yard
27 Drying Yard
28 Infirmary Airing Yard
29 Debtors' Airing Yard
30 Entrance Court
31 Airing Yard, 1st-Class Debtors
32 Airing Yard, 2nd-Class Debtors
33 Airing Yard, 3rd-Class Debtors
34 Gateway
35 Porter's Lodge

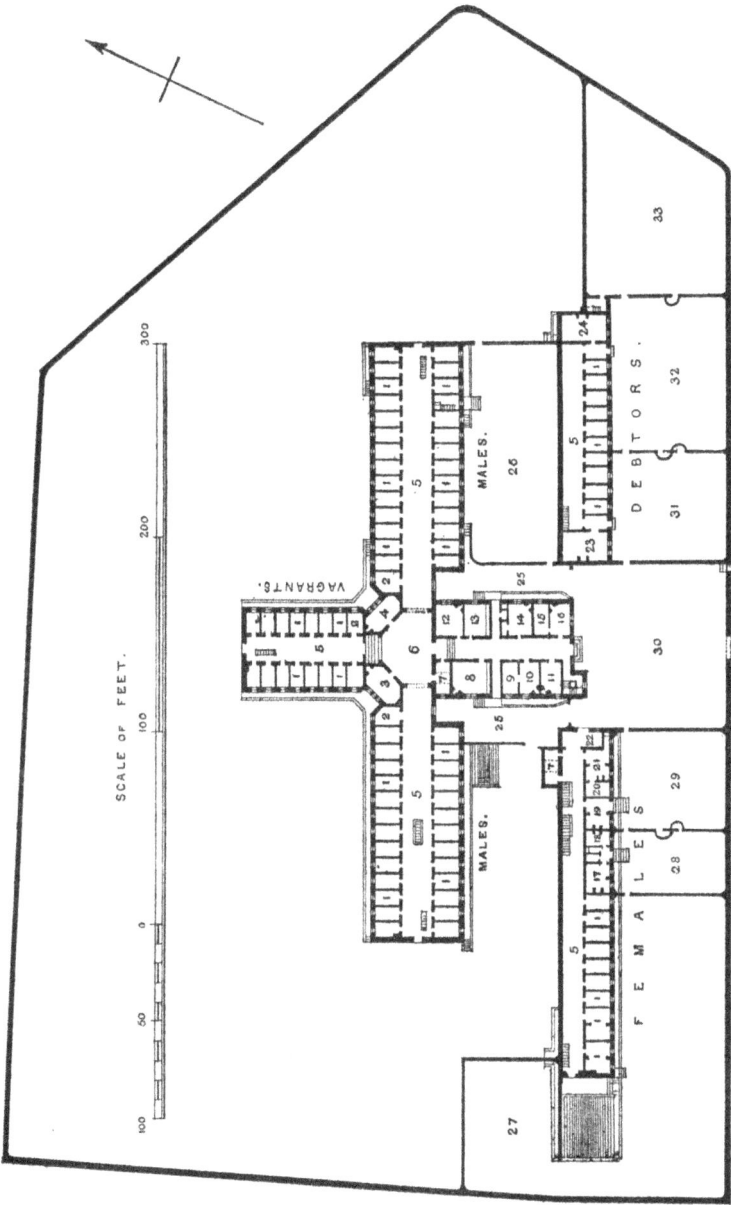

SCALE OF FEET.

100   50   0   100   200   300

MALES.

VAGRANTS.

MALES.

FEMALES

DEBTORS.

CHAPLAINS HOUSE.   GOVERNORS HOUSE.

1 2 3 4 5 6 7 8 9 10 11 12 13 14 15 16 17 18 19 20 21 22 23 24 25 26 27 28 29 30 31 32 33 34 35

A NOTE ON PRISON LITERATURE

There is a large literature on the subject of imprisonment. Memoirs by ex-prisoners are particularly common. The bibliography given here includes many works consulted in the preparation of the present book, but it is intended primarily as a guide for the general reader who wishes to study the causes and treatment of crime and prison conditions today and in the past. Readers without considerable experience in dealing with confirmed criminals would be well advised, when looking at any material written by ex-prisoners, to remember that the majority of such 'memoirs' are written heatedly and resentfully, usually including the most sensational incidents in the authors' experience, and often omitting any reference to positive, helpful treatment they received during their sentences. Moreover, prisons vary greatly in character, and the experience of one man in one or two prisons can never be taken as definitely typical of the treatment of all men and women serving imprisonment.

The author has been greatly helped, in compiling this list, by the staff of the Howard League for Penal Reform, which has an excellent library of penal literature, and by the Librarian of Kent County Library.

I. BIOGRAPHY

CROFT-COOKE, R.: *The Verdict of You All*, Secker & Warburg, 1955.

DENDRICKSON, G., & THOMAS, F.: *The Truth about Dartmoor*, Gollancz, 1952.

GREW, B. D.: *Prison Governor*, Jenkins, 1958.
The autobiography of a man with long and varied experience of prison administration.

HECKSTALL-SMITH, A.: *Eighteen Months*, Wingate, 1954.

HENRY, J.: *Who lie in Gaol*, Gollancz, 1952.

An ex-prisoner's account of her experiences in Holloway Prison, London, and at the open prison for women, Askham Grange, near York.

HIGNETT, N.: *Portrait in Grey*, Muller, 1956.

An account of prison life by a former coroner sentenced for fraudulent conversion. The author seriously under-estimates the idealism of members of the Prison Service, and his general picture of Wormwood Scrubs, where most of his imprisonment was spent, is distorted by bitterness. But it is an interesting companion to Mr Grew's book, which is largely concerned with the same institution at the same period.

HOWARD, D. L.: *John Howard: Prison Reformer*, Johnson, 1958.

An account of the eighteenth-century reformer's life and work.

MAXWELL, R.: *Borstal and Better*, Hollis & Carter, 1956.

NORMAN, FRANK: *Bang to Rights*, Secker & Warburg, 1958.

The memoirs of an ex-prisoner of considerable experience, giving unusual insight into the mind of criminal and the 'hidden society' of prisoners.

PHELAN, J.: *Tramp at Anchor*, Harrap, 1954.

SIZE, MARY: *Prisons I have Known*, Allen & Unwin, 1957.

A personal account of forty-seven years in the Prison Service, many of them as governor of prisons and Borstals for women and girls, with an excellent account of the opening of Askham Grange 'open' prison, of which Miss Size was first governor.

TANNENBAUM, FRANK: *Osborne of Sing-Sing*, University of Carolina Press, 1933.

The life of a distinguished American prison governor.

WHITNEY, JANET: *Elizabeth Fry*, Harrap, 1937.

An excellent biography of this remarkable pioneer.

WILDEBLOOD, P.: *Against the Law*, Weidenfeld & Nicolson, 1955.

A moving and sensitive account of the author's experience in Wormwood Scrubs Prison and of the incidents which preceded his conviction.

II. CAPITAL PUNISHMENT

GARDINER, GERALD: *Capital Punishment as a Deterrent*, Gollancz, 1956.

GOWERS, SIR ERNEST: *A Life for a Life*, Chatto & Windus, 1956.
Each of these books gives a fair account of the cases for and against retention of the death penalty, and submits them to close examination. Sir Ernest Gowers was Chairman of the Royal Commission on Capital Punishment (1954).

Report of the Royal Commission on Capital Punishment: H.M.S.O., 1954.

Report of an Inquiry into the Conviction of Timothy Evans for the Murder of Geraldine Evans: H.M.S.O., 1953.

SILVERMAN, PAGET & HOLLIS: *Hanged . . . and Innocent?* Gollancz, 1953.

TEMPLEWOOD, THE RT. HON. VISCOUNT: *Shadow of the Gallows*, Gollancz, 1951.

III. JUVENILE DELINQUENCY

BRITISH MEDICAL ASSOCIATION AND THE MAGISTRATES' ASSOCIATION: *The Adolescent Delinquent Boy*, London, 1951.

BURT, SIR CYRIL: *The Young Delinquent*, University of London Press, 1948 (4th ed.).
A classic examination of the causes of juvenile delinquency.

CARR-SAUNDERS, MANNHEIM & RHODES: *Young Offenders*, Cambridge University Press, 1942.

COHEN, A. K.: *Delinquent Boys: The Culture of the Gang*, Routledge, 1956.
A study of the sociological causes of delinquency in an American setting.

EDELSTONE, H.: *The Earliest Stages of Delinquency*, Livingstone, 1952.

FERGUSON, T.: *The Young Delinquent in his Social Setting*, Nuffield Trust, 1952.

HENRIQUES, SIR BASIL: *The Home Menders*, Harrap, 1955.

MAYS, J. B.: *Growing up in the City*, University of Liverpool Press, 1954.

PAGE, LEO: *The Young Lag*, Faber, 1950.

STOTT, D. H.: *Delinquency and Human Nature*, The Carnegie Trust, 1950.

Saving Children from Delinquency, University of London Press, 1952.

Unsettled Children and their Families, University of London Press, 1957.

A clear account of Dr Stott's research into family conditions as the origin of delinquency and maladjustment in the child.

WATSON, JOHN: *The Child and the Magistrate*, Cape (rev. ed., 1950). The working of a juvenile court.

IV. CRIMINALS

ABRAHAMSON, D.: *Who are the Guilty?* Gollancz, 1954.

BECKHARDT, J., & BROWN, W.: *The Violators*, Harcourt, Brace & Co., 1955.

EAST, SIR NORWOOD: *Sexual Offenders*, Delisle, 1955.
The Roots of Crime, Butterworth, 1954.

EVANS, JOAN: *Three Men*, Gollancz, 1954.
A sympathetic study of the case histories of three criminal offenders.

PAKENHAM, LORD: *The Causes of Crime*, Weidenfeld & Nicolson, 1958.

PARTRIDGE, R.: *Broadmoor: A History of Criminal Lunacy*, Chatto & Windus, 1953.

PLAYFAIR, G., & SINGTON, D.: *The Offenders*, Secker & Warburg, 1957.

ROSE, GORDON: *Five Hundred Borstal Boys*, Blackwell, 1949.

TRENAMAN, J.: *Out of Step*, Methuen, 1952.
The treatment of military delinquents in England during the war.

V. CRIMINOLOGICAL TEXTS

There are few English textbooks on Criminology directly related to our own penal system and our own social conditions. The work by Howard Jones listed below is the best brief introduction by an English academic criminologist. The others are American

publications, and the very different social background of the
United States and the peculiarities of its penal system should be
borne in mind when they are used.

BARNES, H. E., & TEETERS, N. K.: *New Horizons in Criminology*,
Prentice Hall, 1943.
JONES, HOWARD: *Crime and the Penal System*, University Tutorial
Press, 1956.
RECKLESS, W.: *The Crime Problem*, Appleton-Century-Crofts,
1955.
SUTHERLAND, EDWIN H.: *Principles of Criminology*, Lippincott,
1934.

VI. THE TREATMENT OF OFFENDERS

BENNEY, MARK: *Gaol Delivery*, Longmans, Green, 1948.
CALVERT, E. ROY: *The Lawbreaker*, Routledge, 1945.
EAST, DR NORWOOD, & HUBERT, W. H. DE B.: *The Psychological
Treatment of Crime*, H.M.S.O., 1939.
ELKIN, W. A.: *The English Penal System*, Penguin, 1957.
A survey of the English Penal System in all its aspects, in-
cluding a brief historical account.
EWING, A. C.: *The Morality of Punishment*, Routledge, 1926.
FENTON, NORMAN: *The Prisoner's Family*, California: Atlantic
Books, 1959.
FOX, SIR LIONEL: *The English Prison and Borstal Systems*, Rout-
ledge, 1952.
A classic account of the system and of official policy, by the
present Chairman of the Prison Commissioners.
FRY, S. MARGERY: *Arms of the Law*, Gollancz, 1951.
GLOVER, ELIZABETH: *Probation and Re-education*, Routledge, 1939.
GRUNHUT, DR MAX: *Penal Reform*, Oxford University Press, 1948.
JONES, HOWARD: *Prison Reform Now*, Fabian Society, 1959.
KING, JOAN F. S. (editor): *The Probation Service*, Butterworth,
1958.
An account of the probation service by serving probation
officers, including a description of the basic principles and
methods used in case-work. The main aspects of a probation
officer's duties (enquiries for courts, probation and supervision

of offenders, after-care and matrimonial conciliation) are dealt with in some detail.

KLARE, HUGH J.: *Anatomy of Prison*, Hutchinson, 1960.
MANNHEIM, DR H.: *The Dilemma of Penal Reform*, Allen & Unwin, 1939.
MORRIS, NORVAL: *The Habitual Criminal*, Longmans, Green (Published for the London School of Economics), 1951.
SYKES, GRESHAM M.: *The Society of Captives*, Princeton University Press, 1958.
An impressive sociological study of an American maximum security prison, in which the social roles of custodial staff and prisoners, and the ways in which they interact, are analysed. The situation described in this book is not directly analogous to that existing in English prisons, but the basic problems are relevant to conditions in this country.

TANNENBAUM, F.: *Crime and the Community*, Oxford University Press, 1939.

VII. PENAL HISTORY

ASHTON, JOHN: *The Fleet: Its River, Prison and Marriage*, T. Fisher Unwin, London, 1889.
BATESON, CHARLES: *The Convict Ships, 1789–1868*, Brown, Son and Ferguson, Glasgow, 1959.
BRANCH-JOHNSON, W.: *The English Prison Hulks*, Christopher Johnson, 1957.
GIBB, ERIC: *Incidents of the Convict System in Australasia*, London, 1895.
GRIFFITHS, A.: *Memorials of Millbank*, Chapman & Hall, 1884.
HOBHOUSE, S., & BROCKWAY, F.: *English Prisons Today*, Longmans, Green, 1922.
HOWARD, JOHN: *The State of the Prisons*, Dent (Everyman's Library), 1929.
IVES, GEORGE: *A History of Penal Methods*, Stanley Paul, 1914.
Penal Methods in the Middle Ages.
A work printed for private circulation in 1910, but available in the Library of the Howard League for Penal Reform.

O'DONOGHUE, F. G.: *Bridewell Hospital: Palace, Prison, Schools*, John Lane, London, 1929.

PIKE, L. O.: *A History of Crime in England*, London, 1873.

RADZINOWICZ, L.: *A History of English Criminal Law and its Administration since 1750*, Stevens, 1956.
This work, of which three volumes have appeared so far, is a masterly and remarkably detailed account comprising much original research. The author was appointed first Professor of Criminology at Cambridge University in 1959.

RHODES, A. J.: *Dartmoor Prison, 1806–1932*, John Lane, 1933.

WEBB, SIDNEY & BEATRICE: *English Prisons under Local Government*, Longmans, Green, 1922.

INDEX

For Product Safety Concerns and Information please contact our EU
representative GPSR@taylorandfrancis.com
Taylor & Francis Verlag GmbH, Kaufingerstraße 24, 80331 München, Germany

www.ingramcontent.com/pod-product-compliance
Lightning Source LLC
Chambersburg PA
CBHW050440280326
41932CB00013BA/2190